BUILD A REAL ESTATE CAREER THAT FITS YOU

IAN MAYER

ISBN: 979-8-90252-205-8 (Paperback)
ISBN: 979-8-90252-204-1 (eBook)
ISBN: 979-8-90252-206-5 (Hardcover)

Printed in the United States of America

TABLE OF CONTENTS

DEDICATION

For my wife and kids.

This book is based on my personal experience working in real estate and home inspections. It's meant to share insights, perspectives, and lessons learned, not to serve as legal, financial, or professional advice.

Every situation is different, and real estate laws, practices, and conditions can vary widely by location. Before making any decisions, you should consult with the appropriate licensed professionals for your specific situation.

While I've done my best to provide accurate and useful information, I can't guarantee specific results or outcomes. By using the information in this book, you agree that the author and publisher are not responsible for any decisions made or actions taken based on its content.

All situations are real, but names have been changed. And no, AI didn't write this.

INTRODUCTION

Back in October of 2015, the National Association of Realtors released a report called the D.A.N.G.E.R. Report, and I attended a presentation on it. The report revealed the hard reality about the real estate industry. While the perception is that agents live the good life, like on Million Dollar Listing, Selling Sunset, or other popular TV shows, the truth is far different.

According to the report, 40% of real estate agents never make it past five years in the business. A large percentage of agents only ever sell zero to three homes per year. And every year, roughly 15 to 20% of all agents exit the business for one reason or another.

That is a sharp contrast to the public perception that real estate is an easy career and an easy way to make great money.

Despite the report, very little has changed since then. Yes, the markets have gone way up and way down several times. New brokerages have entered the scene claiming to be better, more cutting-edge. Some older brokerages have faded away and disappeared. And yet, every year, thousands of people get their real estate license, many bright-eyed, picturing easy money, wealth, or at least a better job.

And still, the core problem remains the same.

They get their license, and then they sit there and think, *I've got my license, now what?*

They receive little direction, minimal training, and simply don't know what to do next. One in five will drop out within their first year. Nearly 40% won't make it past five years. Many will quietly fade away without ever having sold a single home.

As someone who works with thousands of agents every year, I can say from experience that the findings are spot on. Even though the report is now well over a decade old, very little has changed. Every year, I meet agents who never get their careers off the ground. I meet agents who seem to be doing well but leave the industry a few years later. I've also met people who were studying for their licenses and eventually became successful, only to walk away from real estate a few years later. And then I meet agents who make a lot of money.

So the question becomes: How do you avoid becoming just another statistic?

My real introduction to the real estate industry came in 2004 when I got a job working for a wholesale mortgage company. I started as an assistant account executive, and then moved into Investor Quality Assurance, where I investigated and fixed loans that had been rejected by Wall Street investors.

During that time, I finally made enough money to put a down payment on a total fixer-upper. The joke was that it had four walls and a foundation. It needed a new roof, new plumbing, and there were holes in the floor so big you could see the dirt underneath. When it rained, my wife and I had to wake up every few hours to empty the buckets we'd placed around the house.

Since then, I've worn several real estate-related hats, including starting a home inspection business from scratch and building it into the most highly reviewed inspection company based in Los Angeles, California. Over the years, I've talked to and worked with well over 6,000 real estate agents, some very up close and personal.

Now you might be thinking: Why would someone who isn't a licensed agent write a book about how to be a real estate agent? Aren't there plenty of books written by actual agents?

Yes, there are. But those books are about what worked for that one person. And you are not someone else. You did not have their parents, their childhood, or their life experiences. You had your own, and they were uniquely yours. So what worked for one person may not automatically work for you. I, on the other hand, have observed what works, and what doesn't, across thousands of agents.

This book isn't about how one person made it in real estate. It's based on watching agents either thrive, or quietly disappear.

Think about this: according to the National Association of Realtors, the average experienced Realtor has eight years of experience and does about 12 transactions a year. That means, on average, an agent will be involved in approximately 96 transactions over their entire career, and even that might be generous, since most agents don't start out doing 12 deals a year.

Now compare that to my perspective. My company works with more than 100 agents in any given month. I've watched people get their licenses and flourish, and I've watched others spin their wheels and eventually leave the industry. I've made it my mission to meet as many agents as possible and observe, without bias, what works and what doesn't.

As someone who's on his own journey through the real estate world, I've learned that while some truths are universal, others are completely personal. What works for one person may not work at all for someone else.

So no, this isn't a "one-size-fits-all" blueprint or a "do-this-and-make-a-million-dollars-guaranteed" type of book. It's not full of fluff and cheerleading that wears off as soon as you put the book down.

This is a practical, real-world guide to building a real estate career around you and your personality. Not another "be just like me" cheerleader.

As Dr. Seuss once said:

"Today you are You, that is truer than true.

There is no one alive who is Youer than You."

Let's build a real estate business that works because it fits you, not someone else's story.

CHAPTER 1

Vision First—Define the Life You Actually Want

Vision.

To start, you need a clear vision of what you want to accomplish in real estate. Too many people start off with, "Well, I just want to make some money." But that's vague. If I gave you a dollar tomorrow, you would have made money. But a dollar is probably not what you were actually thinking.

A vision is: what do you want to accomplish in life? Do you want a house in Encino or a condo by the beach? Do you really want it, or would it just be nice? If it's just nice, then it's not a vision. If you really want it, that's a vision.

Most of us have a hard time with vision. We get asked in countless job interviews, "Where do you see yourself in 5 years?" and most of us come up with, "I see myself helping you get a promotion and getting promoted into your role," thinking we're being clever. But that's not really what the question is asking. It's asking: what is the state of your life in five years?

And the reason many of us struggle with vision starts when we're young. Our parents, teachers, and relatives constantly ask us the same question: *What do you want to be when you grow up?*

Most of us weren't five years old thinking, "One day I am going to be in real estate!" And whatever we might have thought we wanted to be was often met with comments like, "Don't you want to be a doctor or a lawyer?" from our parents or other adults. We struggle with vision because, so often, our visions were shot down when we were kids. Our imaginations were crushed down to fit into tiny, predefined boxes of what other people thought would make us successful.

A better question would have been: What do you want to accomplish in your life? What kind of life do you want to have?

Do you want to own a condo by the beach someday?

Do you want a small ranch on the outskirts of town?

A three-bedroom, two-bath house in suburbia?

A downtown loft where you can walk to shops and restaurants?

Do you want to vacation in Yellowstone? Paris? Both?

Do you want to live simply so you have the freedom to travel the world, or do you want a house so incredible that other people travel to visit you?

Those are the questions most of us never really think about. Instead, we focus on what job we should have rather than what kind of life we're trying to build.

But if you don't know what you're trying to accomplish, then any job will do. And when real estate gets hard, and it will, you'll be tempted to say, "Maybe this isn't for me."

When you have a clear vision of what you're working toward, it becomes much easier to push through the difficult moments.

Cody Sanchez has a line she says she got from her father: *You're not really in the game until you're sitting in the living room in the dark in the middle of the night with your head in your hands, wondering what you're going to do next.*

If you stay in this business long enough, you'll have those moments.

You'll have a transaction that starts spiraling out of control and looks like it might fall apart.

You'll have a stretch where your pipeline suddenly dries up, and the leads stop coming in.

Those moments can and will happen.

If you don't have a clear vision of where you're trying to go, you won't have the motivation to push through them.

Here's an exercise.

Go to the grocery store around five or six o'clock on a weekday evening. Look around for a minute. You'll see people pushing their carts slowly through the aisles, just trying to get through the night. Their mindset is simply, *If I can just make something for dinner, maybe tomorrow will be better.*

You can almost feel how lost they are.

I know, because I used to be one of those people.

I spent years unsure of what I wanted to do next. I was so focused on what job I should have that I never stopped to think about what I was actually trying to accomplish with my life.

Once I shifted that mindset, once I focused on what I wanted to accomplish, the job part suddenly became much easier. I went from switching careers every few years to sticking with one path for more than a decade.

Sometimes motivation comes from unusual places.

There are days I don't feel like going to the gym. But then I remember that grocery store again. I see the seniors struggling to push their carts, careful not to put too much inside because the cart becomes too heavy.

That's where we're all headed eventually.

That thought scares me a little. It scares me enough to go work out. It scares me enough to think about my health and my finances. It pushes me to keep building a career that will support me later in life.

And whenever I'm facing a big decision, I try to run a simple mental exercise.

I imagine myself at eighty years old, sitting in a rocking chair and looking back on my life.

What decisions will I regret?

What chances will I be glad I took, even if the outcome didn't turn out the way I hoped?

When I'm stuck at a crossroads, I try to make the decision that eighty-year-old me would respect.

Because having that clear vision is what carries you through the hard moments, the struggles, the uncertainty, and the times when things simply aren't going the way you planned.

But now, as a real estate professional, it's time to put on your kid glasses, albeit with your now adult lens, and really think: what do I want to accomplish?

Here are two examples from two well-known celebrity agents: Josh Flagg and Josh Altman. Both men are top real estate agents in Beverly Hills, CA, and were stars of the long-running TV show "Million Dollar Listing Los Angeles." Despite both being very successful, they have completely different visions. Yet both use their vision to drive them to be successful.

Josh Flagg's primary vision is to enjoy his life. He likes to travel to Europe and host dinner parties. Josh likes the upscale luxury life. He works hard to fund a life he feels is worth living. However, Josh never builds a team or does anything that doesn't fit his vision for him.

Josh Altman, in his own words, doesn't want to just be the best, he wants to leave no question that he is the best. Altman works very hard to not just fund his life, but to have his name on offices in multiple cities. He works to build large teams of agents under his name. Josh doesn't just think about a nice life; he thinks about legacy and impact that goes well beyond what he can do himself.

Neither is wrong. They are true to themselves. But despite sharing the same first name and having been on the same TV show, their individual visions couldn't be more different.

And this is why you need to be true to yourself in creating your own vision for what you want in life. If you create a vision around the life of Josh Altman, but you don't really want an empire, you will make yourself miserable. If you do not create any vision, you'll meander through the real estate world, sell a few houses, and then quit, as the vast majority of real estate agents do.

One day, a client pulled up to the home I was inspecting in a Ferrari. A really nice Ferrari. We chatted for a few minutes, and he drove off. I thought, "Why don't I have a Ferrari? Why can't I afford a Ferrari?" And it made me think about where my life was heading. Certainly, there was no Ferrari in my immediate future. But after a few days, I realized, I don't want a Ferrari. To me, a fancy car doesn't really motivate me. But having my family live in a nice house and being able to take a nice vacation every year? Now, that's motivating.

A vision is not just something you might want to accomplish someday. It's what you know you will accomplish deep down in your soul. It's what drives you. And without a vision, you will find yourself going nowhere fast.

But before we go on, let's explore why it is so difficult for people looking to get into real estate to establish a career in real estate.

One of the biggest reasons people struggle to transition into real estate has nothing to do with market conditions, competition, or even skill. It has to do with conditioning.

Most people come into real estate thinking it's a job.

Jobs have job descriptions. You show up at a certain time, you sit at a desk, you do assigned work, you take lunch when you're told, and you go home at the end of the day. The structure is built in. Someone else decides what your day looks like.

Real estate doesn't work like that.

Every real estate agent is, by definition, an independent contractor. Most agents *know* this intellectually. But knowing something and actually living it are two very different things.

From the time we're kids, we're trained for structure. Twelve years of school, often sixteen if you include college. Same start time every day. Same lunch period. Same end time. Bells are telling you where to go and when to stop. School is essentially a rehearsal for a traditional job. Even the language is the same, "school day," "workday." Fixed schedules. External authority. Then most of us get a job. Same thing. Someone tells us what time to show up and what time we can leave.

Then you get into real estate, and all of that disappears overnight.

That freedom is the appeal. No boss. No punch clock. No one is telling you when to show up or when you can leave. But the same freedom that attracts people to real estate is the thing that breaks a lot of them.

You see this most clearly with newer agents. They'll refer to their broker or office manager as "my boss," even though legally, and practically, that's not true. A broker can be a mentor, a coach, a sounding board, or even a close friend. But they are not your boss. They can't tell you when to come in. They can't tell you when lunch is. They can't tell you when to go home, and they certainly can't tell you how to run your day.

And yet, when things aren't working, many agents instinctively look *up* instead of inward.

They post online asking whether they should switch brokerages because their broker "isn't doing enough" for them. They assume a different office, a different logo, or a different manager will fix the problem. Sometimes brokerage fit matters, but switching brokerages won't save you if the real issue is that you haven't adapted to being self-directed.

You see a version of this with more experienced agents as well. They come out of the gate hot. They hustle, they build momentum, they stack escrows, they close deals, and they make good money. Then one day, they look up and realize there's nothing in the pipeline. No new clients. No one is pushing them. No one is checking in.

That's when the freedom starts to feel heavy.

They sleep in a little more. Prospecting slips. Not because they're lazy, that's not the right word, but because the external pressure is gone. And slowly, almost quietly, the question creeps in: *Why isn't someone driving me?*

This is why so many agents bounce from brokerage to brokerage, or burn bright for a few years and disappear. It's also one of the biggest reasons most agents don't make it past five years. Their brains never fully adjust to the reality that there is no boss coming to hold them accountable.

So how do you get around this?

First, you have to lean into your why. We'll talk about that in the next chapter, but it matters here because when there's no external structure, purpose becomes the structure.

Second, and this part is uncomfortable, you have to accept that no one is coming to save you.

Not a new brokerage.

Not a new coach.

Not a new market.

Not a new president.

Not a new CRM, system, or course.

Those things can help, but none of them will rescue you.

Personal responsibility isn't optional in real estate, it's the job.

I'll be honest: there are days when I wish I had a boss. Being independent is great most of the time, but that remaining five to ten percent can be brutal. There's no one to hand things off to. No one to say, "Can you deal with this? I don't know what to do." Even with a supportive broker, the weight still lands on you.

But here's the flip side.

Once I truly accepted that no one was coming to save me, something shifted. It was scary at first, but it was also freeing. Because once you take full responsibility for your schedule, your income, and your results, the idea of going back to a rigid, externally controlled job becomes deeply unappealing.

That realization, *I don't ever want to go back*, becomes fuel.

To succeed in real estate, you have to fully buy in. You are your own boss. Your broker can guide you, but accountability belongs to you. You decide your hours. You decide your workdays. You decide when to push and when to rest, and then you hold yourself to those decisions.

Yes, there are times when you hit a wall and need to stop. I've had days where the smartest move was to lie down and reset. But that can't become avoidance disguised as self-care. The bills don't stop. Momentum doesn't maintain itself.

I also had to come to terms with something else: much of what school trained me for was actually a disadvantage in real estate. Being conditioned to wait for instructions. Being rewarded for compliance. Being told when to start and stop. None of that translates well to a business where initiative is everything.

That doesn't mean school was pointless. It just means that you have to accept the rules have changed.

And if you don't consciously unlearn the old ones, they'll quietly sabotage you in this new world.

There's one more thing I rely on, especially on the days when everything feels heavier than it should.

On those days, when I don't feel like dealing with anyone, when the idea of one more call makes me want to put the phone down, I think back to the worst jobs I've ever had. I think about the bad bosses. The ones who yelled. The ones who screamed at me. The ones who took their stress out on me for things that had nothing to do with me and were completely out of my control.

Those memories are surprisingly motivating.

People will sometimes look at me right before I walk into a call space or a tough conversation and ask, "How do you do that?" And what I don't always say out loud is this: fifteen or twenty minutes of discomfort now is infinitely better than eight hours of being yelled at by someone else.

I've lived that life already. I don't want it back.

That perspective keeps me moving on the hard days. Not some abstract vision board or motivational quote, just a very real reminder of what I worked to escape. Freedom doesn't mean the work disappears. It just means you get to choose *which* hard you're willing to tolerate.

And that's an important mental shift.

Sometimes motivation doesn't come from chasing something you want. Sometimes it comes from remembering what you're determined to never go back to. Keeping that front and center helps you stay in the game when discipline wavers and energy dips.

In real estate, mindset isn't about pretending every day is exciting. It's about remembering why this version of hard is still better than the alternative.

From this reality, you can see what happens if you don't set a vision. You can spin in circles as life goes by. With a strong vision, you can set a path to where you really want to go.

My own vision has always been very centered on my family. For me, success was never about flashy things or proving something to the world. My vision has always been about providing for my wife and my kids. Making sure the bills are paid. Making sure the house is secure. Making sure my family has opportunities that maybe I didn't always feel certain about growing up.

That vision carried me through a lot of long days and stressful moments in the early years.

Now that my kids are older, that vision has shifted a little bit. I'm still focused on providing for my family, but I've started thinking more about the next phase of life. I think about retirement. I think about making sure my wife and

I have the resources to enjoy our later years without stress. I think about being able to slow down someday and look back at the life we built together.

Those visions, and the commitment to them, are what keep me going when things get tough.

Fortunately, the good days in this business far outweigh the bad ones. But like any career, there are still difficult days. There are days when a deal falls apart, when something unexpected happens, or when you simply feel worn down.

On those days, I come back to my vision.

Not the job. Not the transaction. The vision.

Because when you're clear about what you're working toward, it becomes much easier to keep moving forward.

I know a few of you are reading at this point and thinking, yeah, that's great, but I am not looking to become a full-time, million-dollar agent. Perhaps this is a part-time career while your kids are in school. Perhaps you're thinking, yeah, I just need a few houses a year for some extra spending money. That is fine. But realize, this is part of your vision. It is okay to be part-time or not have a lofty vision. But not having a lofty vision is still a vision. And you need to keep it in focus, or else, the statistics say, you will not even have that.

CHAPTER 2

Find Your Why (So You Don't Lose Your Way)

Once you've defined your vision, it's time to dig into your why.

Why do you want this life? Why real estate?

People like to say they want to be successful, but they don't define what success means for them. Many assume success means having a fancy car, eating at expensive restaurants, or partying on a yacht. But that's not success, that's simply spending money. If you don't define success for yourself, you'll never recognize when you've achieved it.

Let me go back to that Ferrari moment. After thinking I needed to think bigger, I realized the car didn't matter to me. Even if I could afford a Ferrari, I personally would not buy one. What actually made me happy? Remodeling my house. Saving for retirement. Traveling with my family. That's my why.

And once you know your why, you can align every part of your business around it.

So, then, why real estate?

If your only goal is to make a good income, you could get a job at a fast-food chain and work your way up to manager. You could sell stocks, cars, or any number of things. There are many good-paying careers out there. So why choose a real estate career? Money is a motivator, but if it's your only why, chances are you won't last in real estate.

When I ask successful agents this, their answers vary, but they all have one:

"I love making people's dreams come true."
"I enjoy helping improve neighborhoods."
"I love knowing I helped a family find a home."

The reason your why matters is twofold:

First, when the job gets tough, having a strong why will help you persevere through those moments.

Second, if you can explain why you do what you do to prospective clients, they will be far more willing to do business with you.

This comes straight from Simon Sinek's excellent book Start with Why.

In real estate, the average agent says, "Hi, do you know anyone who wants to buy or sell real estate?" While that might occasionally land a client, it's a generic, impersonal approach.

Compare that to: "Hi, I'm Ann. I am passionate about making families' dreams come true in the North Valley." Even if that's not what the listener needs, it comes across as authentic. And authenticity is everything.

We live in a world saturated with advertising and sales pitches. But the ones that land are genuine. Your why should be felt in every conversation, every post, every listing appointment.

Or, as Maya Angelou said:

"At the end of the day, people won't remember what you said, but they will remember how you made them feel."

This isn't just about a better elevator pitch. A strong why becomes the spine of your brand. It shapes everything that comes next.

For me, I was surprised by how much I fell in love with real estate. I didn't think about it much until my first real estate-related job as an assistant to a mortgage broker. But after just one day, I became obsessed with everything related to real estate.

Why? The answer goes back to my upbringing. I moved six times before I turned six years old, and then again at age nine. I never felt the stability of a solid home as a kid. Everything felt temporary. That shaped me.

Real estate, to me, is about creating that stability for others. I like helping people experience the one thing I didn't have as a young child: a home to call my own.

And I love educating people. That is my real calling.

My personal North Star has always been education, not in the traditional sense of standing in a classroom, but in helping people who genuinely want to learn.

I've never had any desire to become a schoolteacher. Most kids sitting in a classroom aren't there because they want to be educated. They're there because they have to be. That environment never appealed to me.

What excites me is something very different.

I love walking through a house with a potential homeowner and showing them what's really going on with the property. Explaining how the systems work. Pointing out things they might not notice on their own. Watching the moment when it suddenly clicks and they understand their home in a completely new way.

That kind of education is thrilling to me.

It's also something everyone on my team believes in. We don't see ourselves as just inspectors who show up, write a report, and move on. We see ourselves as educators who use the home inspection process as a classroom.

And now I'm taking that idea one step further.

Through this book, I'm doing the same thing, educating people who want to learn. Just like a homebuyer walking through a house, you're here because you're curious, because you want to learn, and because you want to understand how this business really works.

CHAPTER 3

Set Goals or Spin Your Wheels

Once you have a vision, or even a partial one, it's time to set goals.

What's the difference, you may ask?

Vision is your long-term outlook. It gives you direction. It's allowed to shift and evolve as life changes.

Goals, on the other hand, are short-term, measurable, and specific. They're the stepping stones toward your vision.

Let's say your vision is to own a Ferrari when you retire. What model? You might not know yet, and that's okay. Ferrari's lineup could be totally different by then. But if your goal is to buy a Ferrari this year, you need to know the exact model, the price, and how much money you need to save or earn to make that happen.

If your vision is to have a spouse, two kids, and a beautiful home, you don't need to know your future kids' names or the address of the house. But if your goal is to have a down payment saved within 24 months, then you need to know a specific dollar amount.

A vision without goals is just a dream. Goals give structure to your ambition.

Many agents only sell three or fewer houses a year. And truthfully, I've met plenty who are perfectly happy being part-time. Many stay-at-home parents become real estate agents to bring in some extra income, and they're not trying to make this a full-time career. That's totally fine, as long as they're honest with themselves about being content part-time.

But if you want to make real estate your full-time profession, selling zero to three houses a year won't cut it.

The real question becomes:

How many homes do you need to sell to support your vision?

At what price point? With how many clients? In what time frame?

The answer will vary from agent to agent, but defining these numbers is absolutely essential.

Too many agents fall into the trap of not having clear goals at all.

I once led a mastermind lunch with a group of experienced agents. Since it was near the end of the year, I asked everyone what their goal was for the upcoming one. One agent looked at me and said:

"Goal? I just hope to sell more than last year."

Others admitted they didn't really have a goal at all, they were simply hopeful.

Here's the truth:

"More" is not a goal.

"Hope" doesn't pay your bills.

If you don't know what you're aiming for, you're likely to stay stuck in that zero to three transaction range, indefinitely.

There's a quote by Steve Maraboli, which is a twist on a famous line from Alice in Wonderland:

"If you don't know exactly where you're going, how will you know when you get there?"

Successful agents set annual goals.

Some go by the number of units sold.

Others focus on total dollar volume, and most top producers track both.

They adjust those numbers based on market conditions, but they don't guess.

They don't "hope."

They plan.

On the flip side, agents without defined goals just try to "do enough business" to survive, and a large percentage of them don't make it to year two.

Goals can change. And that's okay.

You might hit your initial goal and want to stretch further.

You might get halfway there and realize it's not what you want after all.

That's okay too. The key is being honest with yourself and adjusting your goals in a way that keeps you moving forward, not spinning in circles.

When I first started my home inspection business, my goal was simple:

Make enough to pay the mortgage and buy groceries.

The first time I paid my mortgage using just inspection income, that was a defining moment.

But eventually, that goal wasn't enough. I wanted to fund my retirement. I wanted to provide more for my kids than just food and shelter. I wanted time with my family, not just a way to survive.

So I adjusted my goals. Every year, I re-evaluate.

Sometimes, I adjust halfway through the year. My vision stays consistent, but my goals adapt with the market, the workload, and my own growth.

CHAPTER 4

Hunter or Farmer?

In sales and marketing, there are essentially two styles people tend to gravitate toward: hunters or farmers. Understanding which one you are will help bring massive clarity to developing your marketing plan in the next chapter.

When I got my first job in a true sales organization, they had a one-size-fits-all mentality. You either got on board with their sales plan, or you didn't. And in every sales organization I have ever been a part of, that organization had one style that they expected everyone to follow. It's a shame, though, because not every person is the same. What works for one person may not work for another.

The great thing about the real estate business is that one is allowed to find and develop one's own style. Yes, your broker may have a sales strategy they would prefer you use. Yes, you can go out and purchase a wide variety of books and sales courses, all "guaranteed to work." The issue is that those methods will work if you have a similar personality to the person teaching you their techniques. But you are your own person, not someone else. You need to get in touch with what works for you. Trying to be someone you are not will not only cause you to lose sales, but you will be miserable on top of it.

I first heard about hunter vs. farmer when I took a class on hiring people. They broke down sales into hunters and farmers. Though the concept is not exclusive to them, it explains something I always knew but could never fully articulate about sales and marketing.

What is interesting is that a hunter and a farmer may do some of the same things, but the mentality behind how they do them will be different.

The Hunter

Hunting sales tactics are designed to get immediate results. These tactics are commonly associated with cold calling and direct prospecting. Door knocking is another common hunter activity.

A person who gravitates toward hunting sales tactics loves the thrill of the chase and the feeling of closing a lead. The benefit of a hunter-style mentality in real estate is that they have a much higher chance of gaining and closing their first deal quickly. Because hunters tend to be more aggressive and direct, they simply gain clients faster. This is why many sales organizations outside of real estate design their programs around hunter techniques to close deals quickly.

However, the downside of a hunter is that once a deal is closed, they have to start all over again. Much like a person in the wild who captures a fish, rabbit, or other small game, it's usually only enough for one or two meals, then they have to start again.

The Farmer

Farming tactics are slower-paced. Much like a farmer who tills the soil and plants seeds in the spring, waters and tends to crops through summer, and finally harvests in the fall, farming tactics can take months, if not longer, to produce results.

Think about how long some fruit trees take to grow big enough to produce fruit, some tactics may take years.

The advantage of farming tactics is that, much like a fall harvest, they produce multiple clients to sustain you. You are not one-and-done. As long as you continue to water and tend to the crops, they can keep producing referrals and new clients for years to come.

A Choice?

Now I know what you're thinking: I'll do both. And maybe you will for a time. But while on the surface being a hunter or a farmer seems like a business decision, it is not. It is a decision that will be influenced by your natural personality.

While someone who naturally leans toward farming can be taught how to be a hunter, it will take work. The farmer will need to be taught to push through fears and get comfortable with hunting sales tactics. Yet all the sales classes in the world will not change the fact that a natural farmer will eventually become burned out on hunting. This burnout will either lead them back to farming, or more likely, convince that person that they need a new career in a different field.

Conversely, a natural hunter will get bored with farming sales techniques. Hunters enjoy the thrill of the chase. The process itself is just as exciting as closing an escrow. If there is no chase, the lack of excitement will eventually make them lose interest. Hunters want to feel the success of closing a deal, and waiting months or years for a deal to close doesn't sit well with them. Sure, they can farm, but they just don't enjoy it very much.

And yes, some people will naturally want to straddle the line between the two. Being a hunter or farmer is not an either-or discussion; it's a sliding scale. These are natural tendencies people lean toward. How much a person leans toward being a hunter or a farmer will vary from person to person. The key is to be self-aware of your natural tendencies and understand the pros and cons of each style so that you're not surprised by your results.

Not Sure?

Determining whether you are naturally a hunter or a farmer can often involve complex personality tests. To make it easier, here are a few questions that will help you see which way you tend to lean. Be honest. There is no shame in being either a hunter or a farmer. But knowing your honest self will help your career immensely.

Questions:

When it comes to work, I prefer to have a long-term plan and stick to it, even if it takes time to see results.

Strongly Agree: -1 point
Agree: 0 points
Neutral: +1 point
Disagree: +2 points
Strongly Disagree: +3 points

I enjoy the challenge of closing deals quickly and don't mind the uncertainty that comes with it.

Strongly Agree: +3 points
Agree: +2 points
Neutral: +1 point
Disagree: 0 points
Strongly Disagree: -1 point

I value building lasting relationships with clients and believe that repeat business and referrals are key to success.

Strongly Agree: -1 point
Agree: 0 points
Neutral: +1 point
Disagree: +2 points
Strongly Disagree: +3 points

I'm comfortable patiently nurturing leads and waiting for them to convert into clients or listings.

Strongly Agree: -1 point
Agree: 0 points
Neutral: +1 point
Disagree: +2 points
Strongly Disagree: +3 points

I enjoy the thrill of pursuing new leads and exploring different strategies to generate business.

Strongly Agree: +3 points
Agree: +2 points
Neutral: +1 point
Disagree: 0 points
Strongly Disagree: -1 point

I believe that consistency and reliability in my services are essential to earning trust in the real estate industry.

Strongly Agree: -1 point
Agree: 0 points
Neutral: +1 point
Disagree: +2 points
Strongly Disagree: +3 points

I'm comfortable adapting to different market conditions and rapidly changing circumstances in real estate.

Strongly Agree: +3 points
Agree: +2 points
Neutral: +1 point
Disagree: 0 points
Strongly Disagree: -1 point

At a networking event, I want to meet everyone in the room before I leave.

Strongly Agree: +3 points
Agree: +2 points
Neutral: +1 point
Disagree: 0 points
Strongly Disagree: -1 point

I find satisfaction in long-term projects that require consistent effort and patience to yield results.

Strongly Agree: -1 point
Agree: 0 points
Neutral: +1 point
Disagree: +2 points
Strongly Disagree: +3 points

I'm driven by the excitement of closing deals and the immediate rewards that come with successful sales.

Strongly Agree: +3 points
Agree: +2 points
Neutral: +1 point
Disagree: 0 points
Strongly Disagree: -1 point

Tally Your Score:

25–30 points: You exhibit strong "hunter" tendencies. Your natural inclination is to pursue quick wins, adapt to change, and thrive in fast-paced situations.

10–24 points: You have a balanced approach, displaying traits of both a "hunter" and a "farmer." Your adaptability allows you to excel in a variety of real estate scenarios.

0–9 points: You lean more toward the "farmer" side. You value long-term relationships and consistency in your real estate career.

-1 to-10 points: Your natural tendencies align strongly with being a "farmer." You excel at nurturing leads, building trust, and working patiently toward your goals.

Remember, there are no right or wrong answers. It does not matter whether you lean toward being a hunter or a farmer, what matters is that you are honest with yourself.

Don't Take the Metaphors Too Far

While it's important to understand whether you feel like a natural hunter or farmer, it's just as important to remember that these are only metaphors. Don't take the terminology too far.

Case in point: in Darren Hardy's excellent book The Entrepreneur *Roller Coaster*, a young Darren explains to his mentor how he isn't getting the results he expected from his prospecting efforts. When the mentor looks at Darren's list of prospects, he realizes Darren had titled it his "hit list," a classic example of taking the hunting metaphor too far.

No client wants to be on a "hit list," or "in your scope," or "in your sights." Similarly, no one wants to be treated like a potato or a head of lettuce waiting to be harvested. Your clients are people, and they want to be treated like people. Hunter and farmer are relative terms, not labels to be taken literally.

CHAPTER 5

Discover Your Niche

Once you understand how you naturally operate, whether you're a hunter constantly looking for the next opportunity or a farmer building long-term relationships, the next question becomes obvious:

Where should you focus your energy?

Too many agents try to be everything to everyone. They'll take any listing, any buyer, any price range, any neighborhood, any type of property. On the surface, that sounds flexible. In reality, it usually means they become stretched so thin that they blend into the background.

The agents who build strong, recognizable businesses almost always do the opposite. They become known for something.

Sometimes that means specializing in a certain type of property. Sometimes it means focusing on a particular type of client. Sometimes it means doing a type of transaction most other agents avoid.

The key isn't the niche itself. The key is that once people know what you're good at, they start to remember you when that situation comes up.

Over the years, I've watched agents build successful careers in niches most people would never consider. Some focused on small transactions that other agents ignored. Others focused on very specific communities or types of buyers. And some went straight after the highest-end properties in the market.

Here are a few examples of how different niches can work in the real world.

Marty built almost his entire business around leases. Most agents don't like doing leases because the commission is extremely small, a fraction of what you earn on a typical home sale. Marty realized something important: most agents avoid leases. If he focused on something others didn't want to do, they would send him business.

So instead of prospecting to renters, Marty prospected to other agents.

He would go around his office, and other offices, and simply ask, "Do you have a lease client you'd like to hand off?" In other words, he offered to handle the lease work for agents who didn't want to deal with it.

Most agents were happy to give Marty the business. The clients were still taken care of, and the other agents didn't have to spend time on a small commission transaction. In most cases, they didn't even ask for a referral fee because the amount involved was so small that it wasn't worth the trouble.

So Marty developed a reputation as the lease guy, the person you could hand your short-term clients to so you could focus on larger deals.

By doing ten to twenty leases a month, he was effectively earning the same living as an agent who sold about one average home per month. It was a brilliant example of thinking differently. More paperwork? Yes. But far less stress per transaction. And by focusing his prospecting on other agents instead of the general public, it was much easier to generate business.

Another agent I knew had a similar breakthrough in a completely different niche.

For many years, Sandra was a typical real estate agent. She started once her kids were old enough not to need constant supervision. For years, she moved along, closing three or four transactions annually. Nothing terrible, but nothing remarkable either.

One day, Sandra helped a client buy a mobile home.

Now, many agents avoid mobile homes. The financing is different, and many lenders won't finance them at all. There are numerous rules and regulations that don't apply to traditional homes, and the process can feel unfamiliar if you're used to standard transactions.

But Sandra had the time and resources to figure it out. She learned how the financing worked, how the titles were handled, and how the parks operated. She closed the deal fairly quickly.

Then something interesting happened.

A neighbor in that same park asked if she could list their mobile home. Soon, word spread because Sandra understood the ins and outs of mobile home sales better than most agents. Other agents who didn't want to learn the specialty skills began referring her business. One deal led to another. Before long, she developed a reputation as the mobile home expert.

Where she once completed three or four transactions a year, she was soon closing fifteen, twenty, even twenty-five mobile home deals annually.

Yes, the prices were lower than traditional homes. But because of the higher volume, her income became greater than what she had earned before.

Again, the lesson is simple. Sandra took a type of transaction most agents avoided, learned it thoroughly, and turned it into a thriving niche.

One of the most successful agents I ever worked with, Mary, specialized in senior housing. Her office was located near a large 55-and-over community.

These communities have something most neighborhoods don't: consistent turnover. People move to assisted living, move closer to family, or pass away. At the same time, new retirees are always looking to downsize and enjoy their retirement among peers.

When we first started working together, I was surprised by how many transactions she handled compared to other agents. She worked almost exclusively with clients 55 and older, yet she consistently completed far more transactions than most agents I knew.

Mary also had a colleague, Rich, who worked in the same community. He had technically retired but wanted to stay active. He worked only three days a week, yet because he was a senior himself, residents trusted him immediately. They felt comfortable that he understood their needs. He focused only on seniors and genuinely enjoyed the work.

It wasn't a niche I would have thought of on my own, but for them, it worked extremely well.

Then there's the opposite end of the spectrum: luxury homes.

Luxury homes sell for four, five, sometimes ten times the price of an average house. That means the commissions can also be four, five, or ten times larger.

Many agents assume luxury is something they will "graduate" into after gaining experience. But the truth is, most luxury agents didn't graduate into it. They chose to focus on it.

Luxury transactions are not fundamentally different. The contracts, inspections, and financing challenges are largely the same. The numbers are just bigger.

And that's where many agents struggle. When the numbers increase, so does the pressure. One deal can represent months of income, and that pressure can become overwhelming.

Luxury agents simply don't let that pressure show. They treat a $5 million transaction the same way another agent treats a $600,000 one. They focus on the process, not the paycheck.

Yes, luxury homes can be more complex. They may include guest houses, pools, elevators, and advanced systems. But at the core, it is still the same type of transaction.

The real difference is mindset.

The best luxury agents simply don't let the bigger numbers rattle them. Oh, the $5 million estate didn't close? Well, there is a $10 million estate about to go into escrow. They just don't sweat the numbers. They stay calm no matter what the circumstances are. Not everyone can do that. I get that. But I meet a lot of agents who think luxury agents have some special skills or some kind of voodoo powers to attract luxury clients. And the truth is, they don't. Luxury agents just operate as if the stakes are not a big deal. I'd say the average luxury agent I meet is less upset about a transaction falling out of escrow than the average agent selling average houses.

That's what makes that niche work for them.

A useful exercise when you're trying to define your niche is to imagine your perfect client in detail. Not in vague terms like "a motivated buyer" or "a serious seller," but as a real person. Picture them clearly. How old are they? What kind of clothes do they wear? What kind of car do they drive? What magazines or books would they read? Where do they spend their weekends? The more specific you can make that person, the easier it becomes to shape your marketing around them.

Once you have that ideal client clearly in your mind, direct your marketing toward that person. Write your posts, design your messaging, and choose your platforms with that one individual in mind.

When a coach first suggested this idea to me, I struggled with it. I grew up in San Francisco and went to a very diverse preschool. I still remember a photo from when I was about four or five years old. I'm standing in the middle with two boys on either side of me, both from completely different ethnic backgrounds than mine. I grew up in a mixed-race household, so the idea of defining a "single type" of person to market to initially felt uncomfortable, almost like discrimination.

But after thinking about it more, I realized that was not the point at all. The goal of defining a perfect client was not to exclude people. The goal was to focus.

Trying to market to everyone is overwhelming. When you attempt to speak to every possible client, your message becomes so broad that it ends up connecting with no one in particular. By picturing one specific person and aiming your marketing at them, your message becomes clearer and stronger.

Interestingly, what happens next is almost the opposite of what you might expect. Even though you focus your marketing on one ideal client, the people who respond to you often come from many different backgrounds. They may not all match the exact picture you created in your exercise.

But the focus works. It cuts through the noise, simplifies your marketing decisions, and gives you a clear direction instead of the impossible task of trying to appeal to everyone at once.

CHAPTER 6
Own Your Neighborhood

Whether you pick a niche or are waiting to find one, it is very important that you pick a geographic area to focus on. Most agents don't like to hear this, but narrowing your focus to a specific area on a map for specialization is key to standing out.

Building expertise in a specific area enhances your competitive advantage.

When I ask a real estate agent, "What areas do you serve?" or "What area do you specialize in?" I often get a response like, "I go wherever my clients need me. I don't have a particular area, I don't believe in limiting myself." Or, "I go wherever the wind takes me."

And while that sounds good in theory, what I hear is, "I don't have enough clients to know what areas I serve." Because that's usually the reality.

There's an old saying, one I've heard since I was a kid:

"The three most important things in real estate are: Location! Location! Location!"

It is practically the profession's mantra. And yet, many agents forget to apply it to themselves. But when it is applied, it's often a supercharger to a real estate career.

Case in Point

Sam was just an assistant to another agent when I met him. He hadn't even passed his license exam yet. But after he got licensed, Sam went to work. Within a year, he was selling an above-average number of homes, even compared to experienced agents. He represented so many buyers and sellers that his name became known by every other agent in town. I had multiple agents come up to me and ask, "You know him? How is he more successful than me, even though he's brand new? What's his secret?"

His secret?

He drew a tight circle on a map, about four miles east to west, and seven miles north to south. That was his territory. He researched all the schools in the area and which ones sold spots on their fences for signs. He bought a sign and hung it up at one school. As soon as he closed his first sale, rather than go out and get a fancy car, he reinvested most of his commission into more signs on more schools.

He only worked with buyers and sellers within that area. One time, I stood next to him while he was on the phone with a prospective buyer. The client wanted to buy a neighborhood over. He said, "I can't help you then, you'll need to find someone else." I was stunned. He turned down a sure commission just to stay inside his territory. And yet, it paid off.

Soon, he had a sign on every school within his defined area. You literally could not drive through the area without seeing one of his signs. After being on every schoolyard, he reinvested his commission checks in signs on the local grocery store carts. Again, not leaving his well-defined area. He simply became the face of a neighborhood.

Sam became one of the highest-producing agents in terms of volume in a short time. His face was everywhere. People who didn't know Sam felt like they knew him. When he called another agent about showing their listing to his buyer, they already knew who he was. That's what happens when you go all-in on a specific territory: you don't just work the neighborhood, you become the neighborhood.

Another Example

Sandy is a long-time agent who always seems to have either a buyer in escrow or a new listing. The minute one house closes, she's already announcing another one. It's stunning, year after year; she's never more than a few days without either an escrow in progress or a new listing. What is her secret? I wondered. Magic lead generation? A magic CRM? It can't just be luck; luck will only get you so far.

One day, I sat down to figure it out. How was Sandy so successful when so many others were not? When it hit me, I almost fell out of my seat. I realized that every house she had ever sold, as a buyer's agent or as a listing agent, was all in the same neighborhood. In fact, most of her deals were within walking distance of one another, many on the same street.

Her success was a mix of flyers and postcards to the neighborhood after every deal, along with old-fashioned door knocking and a few well-placed signs. Sandy owned this neighborhood. Every potential seller saw her name so often attached to a sale that they just called her. Even buyers noticed she was everywhere within that well-defined neighborhood. She knew all the houses.

Sandy and Sam also had something in common: they lived in the center of their neighborhood. They weren't just representatives of the area; they were part of it.

Most of the highly successful agents I know have clearly defined territories. That doesn't mean they never work outside their zone, but they stay focused. They don't spread themselves thin chasing deals all over the map.

Mary, someone I consider a dear friend, never planned to get into real estate. In fact, for most of her adult life, she had been fully dedicated to raising her kids and supporting her husband's career. Real estate was never on her radar.

But then life took a hard left turn.

Mary's husband fell seriously ill. Suddenly, she found herself in a situation she hadn't expected, needing to support the household. Mary didn't have time to dabble or figure things out slowly. She needed a career that could produce income quickly. So she studied hard, passed her real estate exam, and hit the ground running, not with some city-wide campaign or huge social media blitz, but by focusing on a single, tightly defined community: 1,290 homes and a few surrounding blocks. That was it.

Mary didn't have fancy branding. She didn't have a big team; she didn't even belong to a big brokerage. What she had was focus, relentless focus. She got to know every street, every floor plan, and every pattern of when people moved in and out. She made herself known, not by shouting, but by showing up consistently and with care.

Despite working in such a small area, she quickly tripled the number of transactions that most agents do in a year. Triple.

Why? Because she wasn't wasting time driving across the county. She wasn't trying to be everywhere. She was not trying to impress everyone. She was always right there outside the gates of this senior community, present, available, knowledgeable. The people in that neighborhood began to trust her. They saw her as one of them. And they responded to that.

Mary built a full-time career out of a tiny sliver of the potential market because she committed to her sliver fully, and because she had to. It's one of the most inspiring and quietly powerful examples I've ever witnessed of what can happen when someone leans into one community and says, "This is mine."

Stories like hers are exactly why I believe that defining your territory isn't a limitation, it's a launchpad. And once you've got traction in one area, everything else becomes easier: marketing, referrals, time management, and your reputation.

As I said, this does not mean you cannot do business elsewhere. Randy, another top agent I know, only markets in a single town that is approximately 17 square miles. He regularly works with buyers and sellers all over Los Angeles. But he only advertises in his target area. All of Randy's marketing, ads, videos, and materials only mention that he works in his target area. It defines his business.

Yet, I still see most agents claiming they will go anywhere. I often hear, "I go wherever the wind takes me." And usually, the wind will blow you off a cliff if you're not careful, which is why so many real estate agents are not successful.

My Own Experience

When I started my business, one of the first things I did, before I had clients, before I had branding, was draw boundaries on a map. Literal lines. I made honest assumptions about how far I could reasonably drive and still have enough time in the day to do quality work, follow up, and not burn out.

Occasionally, I would take jobs outside those areas, and every time, I'd be stuck in traffic on the way home, regretting taking the job, realizing I could have done two jobs in the same amount of time it was taking me to do this one.

Even now, with a full team of inspectors and multiple support staff, we still base our advertising and job acceptance on what makes sense geographically, from each inspector's home base. We don't just send people wherever the phone rings. We ask, "Is this a good use of time? Can this be done efficiently without overloading our team or spreading them too thin?" Because doing quality work and maintaining sanity both matter.

That's why it always blows my mind when I see brand-new real estate agents advertising that they'll go anywhere in Southern California. Like, really? Anywhere? That's insane. Between traffic, mileage, and the simple reality of this region's geography, it's nearly impossible to cover that kind of territory effectively as a one-person operation.

It's not just about physical exhaustion, it's about opportunity cost. Every hour spent on the freeway is an hour not spent showing another home, meeting a new client, following up on leads, or building your presence in a specific area. And trust me, no one remembers the agent who's "everywhere." They remember the agent who's always around here.

Why Narrowing Your Territory Works

So why does working a defined geographic territory outperform the "go anywhere" strategy?

1. You Become a True Expert

The smaller the area, the easier it is to learn everything about it: real estate trends, neighborhoods, schools, restaurants, even the housing styles. Over time, you'll know the layouts before stepping inside. You'll walk into homes already familiar with their quirks, and that impresses clients.

You'll also know the history of sales in the area. If you show a lot of homes in one neighborhood, eventually, you'll have been inside most of them. You'll know the houses, and the people.

2. You Win the Listing Appointment

Imagine two agents going for the same listing. Same age, same years in the business. Each has five sales under their belt.

Agent 1: All five sales are in this seller's neighborhood. They can say, "I sold one two blocks over, one three blocks over, another just down the street…" They know the neighbors and the housing styles.

Agent 2: Same five sales, but spread out across town, or even cities apart. They've never been inside the seller's neighborhood before today.

All else being equal, who's the seller going to hire? Right, the neighborhood expert.

3. Targeted Marketing

Going back to Chapters 6 and 7, when you have a defined area, you can tailor your content. Messaging, branding, social media posts, and even postcards become more effective when you're speaking directly to one community.

And remember, in real estate, it's not just who you know. It's who knows you. Referrals are easier to generate when people associate you with a specific neighborhood.

4. Better Time Management

Now imagine you're representing a buyer three hours away. Every showing? Three hours each way. When escrow opens? Another six-hour round trip for inspections, appraisals, walk-throughs, and repairs.

That's a ton of wasted time you could've spent helping more clients. Working locally means you can offer better service and faster turnaround. Clients notice that, and they refer you more often.

5. You Can Scale

When you start juggling multiple clients, geography becomes a major factor. If everyone's in your zone, it's easy to:

Prospect in the morning
Show homes to one client mid-day
Show a second home in the afternoon
Meet a third client in the evening

You can even book back-to-back showings at your own listings.

But if your clients are scattered all over the county, you'll burn yourself out trying to get from one to the next. And clients can tell when you're spread too thin; they feel it.

Bottom Line

If you want to become a high-volume agent, you must define your geographic territory.

This isn't about limiting yourself; it's about maximizing your impact. When you specialize in one area, you:

Build trust
Gain authority
Save time
Market smarter

Handle more clients without losing your mind

Choosing the Right Territory

Start with the neighborhood you live in, or the one you want to live in. When you've got a vested interest, your passion comes through. Clients pick up on that, even if it's subconscious.

And passion is contagious. It gives you the edge over agents who just show up with a data sheet and no real connection to the community.

CHAPTER 7

Choose Your Marketing Method and Dominate It

After you've given some thought to whether you lean toward hunting or farming, a niche, and a neighborhood, it's time to choose one to three primary marketing methods. I say a few because not everyone is going to enjoy every method, and there's only so much time in a day.

Too many real estate and sales gurus say, "Do what I do, and you will succeed." But you're not them. You're you. You need to pick what will work for you, the way your brain works and what you are comfortable with. Work can be hard, but you need to pick the hard you can deal with.

Every method in this book has been proven to work by some agents. And every method in this book has also been dismissed by others who didn't see results. I talk to agents all the time: one will say, "Open houses are great, cold calling never gets me a lead," and the very next agent will say, "Open houses are a drag and a waste of time, cold calling is the key to success."

So who's right?

They both are, for themselves.

That's why the key to actual success is defining what's going to work for you, not what worked for someone else.

No "Toe Dipping"

Once you've chosen your strategy, or strategies, the next step is to go all in. No toe dipping.

What do I mean by "toe dipping"? It's when you say, "I'm just going to try this method for a while and see how it goes." If that's your mindset, odds are that method will fail.

If you don't fully commit and only experiment, you won't get far. For example, if you decide to try cold calling and make twenty calls a day for two days, you'll probably end up with nothing to show for it. If you sit at an open house two Sundays in a row and decide it's not "your thing," chances are you won't have many leads.

That's toe dipping, just testing the waters.

And the problem with toe dipping is twofold:

You're competing against others who've gone all in on the same method. Clients can feel your hesitation and will likely choose another agent who gives off a fully committed vibe.

Now, if you want to toe dip just to see if you enjoy a method, that's fine. Go ahead. Just don't expect much success from it. But once you figure out your method, you have to go all in with all your might, as if your life depends on it. Because, okay, you won't die, but your career will if you don't go all in.

Common Methods Real Estate Pros Use to Get Leads

This is not meant to be an all-inclusive list. And most of these you are probably already aware of. But have you chosen specific methods? And do you stick to them?

Cold Calling

Since the invention of the telephone, salespeople have used it to reach out to potential clients. Yes, people now have caller ID, they screen calls, and it's harder than it used to be, but cold calling still works for some agents.

The key? Set a number, like fifty, and call that many people a day, four to five days a week. Yes, you'll hit a lot of voicemails. Yes, you'll get hang-ups. Yes, you'll even get the occasional angry caller. But if you stick with it, it works.

Pro tip: Have a mirror in front of you and smile while you call. Even though people can't see your face, they can hear whether you're smiling in the tone of your voice.

Warm Calling

Warm calling can be used alongside cold calling or as a stand-alone method. The difference? Warm calls are to people you've had previous contact with, or to people who are expecting your call because someone else mentioned you.

For example, you tell your friend Bob that you're now a real estate agent. Bob says, "Oh, my friend Gina is looking to sell her house and move to a condo." You say, "Great. Can you call Gina and set up an introduction?" He does, Gina agrees, and now you're calling her with context. That's a warm call. You've been introduced. There's a connection.

Anyone you've spoken to before, even briefly, can be considered a warm call.

I worked with an agent who was closing a sale every single month. I asked him how he was outpacing so many more experienced agents. He said he made fifty calls a day, every day. Past clients, future prospects, people he hadn't spoken to in a week, it didn't matter. He kept a notepad with "50" written at the top and made his calls throughout the day until he had fifty checkmarks. That was his system.

And it worked.

Open Houses

Open houses are one of the oldest and most reliable ways to meet clients. You're sitting at a house, meeting people who are curious, and hoping one of them is a future lead.

And here's the secret: you're not really looking for someone to buy that house. You're looking for someone who wants to buy a house and doesn't have an agent yet.

If you don't have your own listing, borrow one. Get to know the other agents in your office. Even the most experienced agents can't sit at all of their listings every weekend. They'll often be happy to let someone else from the office cover an open house.

And if nobody in your office has one, call other offices. It's not unusual for an agent from a different brokerage to sit at an open house, as long as the listing agent gives permission. Most listing agents would rather have someone host an open house than have the home sit empty.

At the open house, your job is to talk to people, get their information, and follow up. A phone call afterward works best: "Hey, you came by the house at 123 Main Street, are you still looking? Want to see something else nearby?" If you don't get people's information, you may as well not have bothered.

Door Knocking

Door knocking, another tried-and-true method used by real estate professionals. Much like cold calling, it puts you in contact with people you do not know. But instead of using the phone, you're literally walking up to their door and talking to them directly, face to face.

What you don't want to do is pick a large, random area and hit it once. That won't produce results. Instead, pick a well-defined area or neighborhood and commit to knocking on the same homes every two to three months. Over time, you'll become known as the "local real estate expert." Sure, some people will groan and hide. Some will be mildly annoyed that you're knocking yet again. But others will be happy to see you. And most importantly, someone will be thinking, "Yes, I'm going to sell soon. I'll call that agent who keeps stopping by."

Eventually, yes, you will get a lead. And yes, that lead will turn into a sale.

A True Story

Once, my neighbor decided to sell. Her kids had grown and moved out. The house was too big, and she was ready to relocate. She asked me for a recommendation, so I gave her the names of three agents I felt matched her personality.

She called one of them and never called the other two.

Instead, she hired the agent who had door-knocked her house that week. That agent not only got the listing and closed the sale, but the buyer of that home used the same agent again a year later to sell it. One door knock turned into two sales. That's the power of door knocking, if you stick with it.

The Notepad

This method involves dropping off notepads, or another trinket with your branding, at homes in a neighborhood without knocking. It's less intrusive, and you can even hire someone else to distribute them.

The downside? No real connection. I used to get five to ten notepads a month. I used them for scrap paper, sure, but I didn't feel connected to any one agent, especially when multiple notepads arrived at once. I do not see much value in leaving notepads unless it's part of a bigger plan.

Some agents go big just once a year instead of every few months, like pumpkins at Halloween or flags on the Fourth of July. One agent always puts a flag in front of my house every Independence Day like clockwork. These agents do find moderate success, but it's not the most effective strategy. Yes, it gets your name out there, but not on a personal level.

Postcards

Postcards can work, but they're expensive. This is not a strategy for new agents unless they have deep financial backing.

Daisy is an agent who works in my neighborhood. Every two weeks, I get a postcard from Daisy. Why me? I have no intention of selling. But the cards keep coming, every two weeks. The thing is, when I drive around my neighborhood, I constantly see a house for sale with her name on it. I finally met Daisy at a networking event. She told me she has narrowly defined areas, and she sends every single house in that area a postcard every two weeks. I just happened to be in the middle of her area. She admitted that it's a very expensive way to market herself. Yet, for her, it works. She gets just enough listing appointments to justify spending the money.

Where most agents fail is by sending one round of postcards and waiting, or two rounds, and then quitting. That won't work. You must do this consistently over time. Occasionally, I get a postcard from an agent that is not Daisy. They look almost silly in comparison. "Hi, I sold one house down the street from you." Or it's a list of houses that just happen to be for sale in the area, and then silence. Maybe a second card, but almost never a third. Why bother if you are not going to be consistent?

The Follow-Up After a Sale

Once you've made a sale in a neighborhood, whether you're the listing or buyer's agent, you follow up with the surrounding neighbors. Ideally, this is done in person through door knocking, paired with a flyer. Postcards can work too, but door knocking adds a personal touch.

You introduce yourself and say, "I just represented your neighbor in the sale of this home." This builds instant credibility.

The key: strike while the iron is hot. Go within days of the closing and only hit homes in close proximity, within a few blocks. Obviously, the drawback is that you need a sale to start with.

Networking

Of all the strategies here, networking is the most universal. It applies to every business, not just real estate. People do business with people they know, and the only way for them to know you is to show up.

Start with your local Chamber of Commerce. Join networking groups. Attend breakfasts, mixers, and fundraisers. Don't just go once, go consistently.

The mistake most people make is showing up once, handing out a few cards, and disappearing. Regular attendees will quickly spot a "one-and-done." The goal is to become a familiar face.

When I first built my business, networking was key. I showed up, met people, and got to know my community. It was organic, it was real, and it worked. Eventually, I got too busy to network, but once I grew my team, I got back into it. And it's still effective.

Just remember: bring a card and a smile.

The Community Ambassador

This approach is all about getting involved, school events, charity fundraisers, cleanup days, street fairs. Be visible. Be helpful. Be known.

Think of it like this: if you're showing up regularly in the same community spaces where your potential clients live, work, and raise their families, you stop being "just another real estate agent." You become their real estate agent, someone they recognize and trust long before they need you.

You don't have to be the loudest person at the event, but you do have to be consistent. Volunteer to set up tables at the school carnival. Donate snacks for the youth soccer team. Sponsor a local 5K run or pitch in at a neighborhood beautification day. Hand out water bottles with your branding at summer festivals. None of this is about a hard sell, it's about building relationships and showing that you're invested in the community for the long haul.

The agents who thrive as community ambassadors are the ones who genuinely care. They know the name of the PTA president. They show up to support local businesses on Small Business Saturday. They've met the neighborhood council representative. They're the person people think of when someone says, "Hey, do you know a real estate agent?"

This strategy doesn't deliver instant gratification. It is a very long-term method. But over time, your name becomes familiar, and familiarity breeds trust.

And when someone's ready to sell their home or buy their next one, they're more likely to call the person who's already shown up for their community, you, than someone they've never met.

School Banner Ads

One related strategy is buying banner ads at local schools. Many schools raise funds by renting space on fences. This can be successful if done right.

I already told you the story of Sam. He proved banner ads can be very effective, particularly if you target multiple schools.

Bus Stop Benches

You've seen them. A bus stop bench with an ad on it. Agents love to buy bus stop ads. Most research studies I've seen claim this is not an effective strategy, and I do not see it being effective.

There are two bus stop benches near my house. Same route, same stops. If you've driven through my neighborhood more than once, you've probably seen them. For the past eighteen years, yes, eighteen, the same two real estate agents have had ads on those same two benches.

Every now and then, they refresh the ads. The sun-worn, fading pictures get replaced with a new copy of the same ad. But the ads themselves have never changed. It's the same two pictures, year after year.

Here's the odd part: in nearly two decades of living here, I've never once seen their names on a listing. Not on a sign rider, not in the MLS, not on a flyer at an open house. I have never met a client who used them. I have never bumped into them at a broker caravan or any real estate event, and I go to a lot of events. It's like they exist in a parallel real estate universe that never intersects with mine, or anyone else's that I know. And worse, they are side by side, competing with each other for your business.

And yet, those ads are always there, like clockwork. I assume they work enough to keep renewing the space, bench advertising isn't free. But if you asked me to name five top-producing agents in this zip code, neither one would make the list. People call people they know and feel like they can trust, not people they see at a single bus stop. If you insist on doing a bus stop ad, it needs to be part of a bigger marketing plan, not your primary method.

Calendars

Another well-loved strategy I see agents use is distributing calendars that have their name and contact information on them.

My basic thought comes down to how many times I have been in a home with an agent's calendar on the wall, and that agent is not representing the sale or the buyer. Other than their picture hanging on the wall, they have nothing to do with the transaction. Let me tell you, I have been in thousands of homes where an agent's face was hanging on the calendar in the kitchen, yet that agent was nowhere to be found in the transaction. To me, that says calendars sound like a great marketing tool, but they are not effective.

I have only met one agent who ever told me calendars worked for them. But this agent had thirty years in the business with hundreds of past clients to whom she could give calendars. For her, calendars were not prospecting for new clients; rather, they were simply a method of staying in contact with past clients should they need to sell or buy again. And even with her stated success, I wouldn't consider her a top agent. Again, calendars should only be part of a bigger plan and not solely relied upon.

Paid Leads

There are numerous websites and companies that will supply you with leads for a price. New ones pop up all the time, and others fade away.

Overall, I'm not a fan of paying for leads. First, the leads tend to be people who have no reason to want to work with you specifically, and therefore may not always convert. The other issue with paid leads is that they can cost significant amounts of money. I've heard from so many agents that by the time they get a deal to close and receive their commission check, and then subtract the cost of the lead, they really didn't make much of a profit.

CHAPTER 8

Social Media

Social media.

Regardless of which method you use from the previous chapter, you have to follow it up with social media. It's that important. In fact, some agents build their entire business around social media first, and everything else second. That's up to you. But either way, you need to have a presence.

Most buyers today will check your social media. They want to verify you. They want to see if you're the real deal. Social media has basically become the new business card. If you're not on social media, a lot of people will assume you don't exist.

And yes, I've heard it before: "I don't want to put my private life out there." "I'm not trying to be a star." "I don't want everybody knowing my business."

Well, I've got bad news: then you're in the wrong business. You're not going to succeed in real estate unless you're willing to put yourself out there. Because like it or not, as a real estate agent, you are a mini celebrity. You may only be a celebrity within your farm, your client circle, or your niche, but that's still celebrity status in that space. And you need to treat it that way.

Now, that doesn't mean you need to spill everything like a reality TV contestant. Nobody needs a full exposé of your personal life. But you do need to show up and be visible.

I'm not going to tell you which platform to use. I've been teaching social media to agents for over a decade, and what works is always changing. Features change. Algorithms change. Entire platforms come and go. If I gave you a list of tactics today, they might be outdated by the time you read this.

What doesn't change is this: social media is here to stay, and it's critical to your business.

So naturally, the question becomes: "How often should I post?"

Answer: as often as possible.

When I was starting out, my goal was to post once a day, five to six days a week. As I got busier, it became multiple times a day, every day of the week. Yes, seven days a week.

I've heard it all: "I posted once or twice, and nothing happened." Of course not. A single post is like a snowflake. One snowflake hits the ground, no one notices. But if it keeps snowing, day after day, it starts to accumulate. Suddenly, you've got a blizzard.

Social media works the same way. One post won't change your business. But consistent posting over time will.

When people tell me social media doesn't work, I ask how long they've been consistent. The answer is usually a week or two. You have to play the long game. It may take months, or even years, to build a following that turns into business. But it works.

I remember about two years into my career, someone stopped me and said, "Hey, I see you online. You're that guy." That's when it hit me: it's working. And during COVID, when face-to-face networking disappeared, social media carried us. We grew while many others didn't, because we stayed visible.

Now I know what some of you are thinking: "But I don't have anything to post."

Yes, you do. Even when I only had one inspection a week, I found ways to post every day. I'd take multiple photos from different angles and spread them out across the week. People thought I was busier than I actually was.

Agents can do the same thing. If you have a listing, don't just post everything at once. Break it up. One day it's the kitchen, the next day the bathroom, then the backyard, then the street view. Spread it out.

If you don't have a listing, use someone else's, with permission. Post something like, "This isn't my listing, but I'd be happy to show it to you." Just be clear. Most agents are fine with that.

"But why pretend I'm busy?" Because people want to work with agents who appear active. Busy agents get hired. Agents sitting at home scrolling do not.

You can also post about daily life. People don't understand what real estate agents do all day, so show them. You're at your desk, on the phone, in your neighborhood, working. Let them see it.

Have a buyer? Show it. One agent I know once posted a map of all the homes she planned to show that day. Another posted, "Here's the home I'm showing today." Simple, but effective.

Even paperwork is a photo op. Most clients don't realize how much paperwork real estate involves. A quick photo of you working through forms shows you're doing the behind-the-scenes work.

If you're in escrow, jackpot. You can post about inspections, the termite report, the title rep, the process itself. Escrow is a goldmine for content. And don't worry if a deal falls through, most people won't notice.

You can even post about continuing education. I've taught social media classes where I beg people to post that they're there, but most don't. Why? That's gold. You're showing you're sharpening your skills. Why not document that?

And every now and then, yes, make a personal post. No, not a tell-all, but something real. If you're a parent, share something another parent might relate to. If you ride motorcycles or play music, talk about that. It creates a connection.

Years ago, I hesitated to mention I was once a struggling musician. I thought it made me look like a failure. But it turns out, tons of people here are former musicians. It gave us common ground. That's the power of sharing.

Now, don't get caught up in platform specifics. But do pay attention to trends. If a new format is gaining traction, check it out. You don't have to be an expert, just be aware.

Most of all, be yourself. People can smell fake from a mile away. You're not the right agent for everyone, and that's fine. The right clients will connect with the real you.

Let's talk open houses. Going to host one? Post about it, before, during, and after. Even if it's not your listing, you're there working. Let people know.

Some agents are afraid it'll attract the wrong kind of attention, but you want attention. That's the whole point.

If you're printing flyers or postcards, post those graphics too. Why spend money on marketing materials and then not use them online?

Door-knocking today? That's content. Shoot a quick video on the street. That's hustle. Show it.

Bottom line: just post something. Posting something is always better than posting nothing.

Remember, if someone checks your social media and you haven't posted in months, they'll assume you're no longer active, even if they just met you. Social media isn't just advertising. It's proof of life.

Now, how many platforms should you be on? As many as you can manage. Pick two or three to go hard on, and for the rest, post and let it fly. But the ones you interact on, that's where you'll get results.

Don't just post and disappear. Respond to comments. Acknowledge people. Start conversations.

A lot of people think, "Okay, but my friends and family know I am a real estate agent, why remind them?" Because the fact is, most of your friends, and even many of your family members, will not remember. Most people are so wrapped up in their own lives, their own problems, their own careers, they're not thinking about yours. If you do not remind them of what you do, they can and will forget.

Have you heard of the term CEO, Chief Executive Officer? Or COO, Chief Operating Officer? Well, you are now the CRO of you. You are the Chief

Repeating Officer of the company of you. You need to stand loud and proud and repeat what you do for people to remember.

To wrap it up: I don't know a single super-successful real estate agent without a social media presence. Not one.

Renaldo was doing okay as an agent. He landed his first transaction within six months of getting his license. He was working with his friends, people in his community, and his church to get leads. Then one day, he started posting about showing houses, opening escrow, the home inspection, the termite inspection, and everything else that went into the sales process. He found he was getting multiple direct messages from people about the process. He said many comments were along the lines of "Wow, you really care about your clients" and "Thank you for showing how it really works." Many of these messages turned into future clients.

CHAPTER 9

Beware of the Real Estate Market Waves

One of the hardest things about real estate isn't the clients, the contracts, or even the chaos. It's the market itself.

The real estate market moves in cycles. Sometimes it's up. Sometimes it's down. When it's up, everything feels easy. Deals fall into place. Phones ring. You start to believe you've cracked the code. When it's down, it can make you question everything, your skill, your judgment, even whether you belong in the business at all.

I learned that lesson the hard way.

In 2021, the market was on fire. I was riding high. I was hiring inspectors, and every time I hired another one, our production increased. Revenue went up. Stress went down. Everything seemed to confirm that I had mastered the game. I drifted off into other projects, wrongly thinking I was much better at leading a company than I was.

Then, toward the end of 2022, it felt like hitting a streetlight in the middle of the freeway at full speed.

The market shifted fast. Transactions slowed dramatically. I quickly realized something uncomfortable but important: I wasn't nearly as brilliant as I thought I was. I hadn't mastered the market, I had been riding a great wave.

I wasn't the only one to feel this way. In the months prior, there were agents boasting that if they just put their sign up in your front yard, they could sell your house. Agents' egos were getting big, and many thought they had mastered listings through no real strategy other than existing. They were not lying, they could in fact sell a house fast with just a sign; however, it was not that their sign was anything special. Every agent at the time was experiencing the same up market. And just like I did, many agents got humbled very fast when the market went down. Good agents adjusted, took their humble pie, and shifted strategy. Many others simply got out of the game, let their license expire, and got a different job.

That realization stings, but it's valuable. Because once you understand that markets rise and fall, you stop tying your identity to whether conditions are favorable. You start focusing on what you can control.

Here's what too many agents get wrong. Even in a down market, especially in a down market, real estate is still moving. Houses are still being bought and sold. Life doesn't pause just because interest rates go up or headlines turn negative.

The worst excuse I hear from agents who aren't producing is, "Well, it's a slow market."

Yes, the market may be slow. That's not the same thing as dead.

You've probably heard about the "four Ds": death, divorce, debt, and downsizing. Some add a fifth D for displacement or relocation. These are common reasons people move, and they don't disappear when the market slows down.

Let's actually talk about them.

First, death.

As uncomfortable as it is, people pass away every single day, regardless of what the market is doing. When someone inherits a house, or when a surviving spouse no longer wants, or emotionally can't stay in, the home, the market is not their primary concern. They're dealing with loss and logistics. They suddenly have a property they don't need.

When my mom passed away, I wasn't wondering whether it was a good time to sell. I was faced with the reality that I had a house to deal with. I didn't want to live in it. I didn't want to manage renters. I needed someone to help me sell it and move on. That's it. The market wasn't part of the equation.

That situation happens every day of the year. Even in the worst downturns, someone is inheriting a house they need to sell.

Next is divorce.

I watched this happen with a house down the street from me. A couple bought it, remodeled it, moved in, and everything looked perfect. A few months later, it was back on the market. They were divorcing.

Nothing was going to keep them in that house. It didn't matter what the market was doing. They needed to sell, and they needed to sell quickly.

I don't know anyone who thinks, "Yeah, I'm going to stay married until the market changes." When it's over, it's over. That creates transactions in every type of market.

Then there's debt and financial pressure.

This can show up more visibly in down markets, but it exists in every cycle. People lose jobs. Medical bills pile up. Sometimes they simply realize they're overextended, too many payments, too much stress.

For many, selling the house becomes the cleanest way to reset. No more mortgage payments. Possibly some equity to eliminate other debts. Even when someone is upside down, selling is often better than foreclosure. Financial pressure is one of the strongest motivators in real estate, and it never fully disappears.

Then there's downsizing.

Kids grow up and leave. People retire. Lifestyles change. None of this follows market cycles. When your children move out, you don't wait five years for ideal conditions. When you retire, you retire when it's right for you.

For years, I worked with a retirement community in Santa Clarita and did hundreds of inspections there. Why? Because there was always someone ready to move into a smaller place. That demand didn't vanish when the market softened. It never has.

Now think about upsizing and birth.

People try to plan their lives perfectly, but kids happen when kids happen. You can't time a pregnancy to interest rates. You have nine months, and the market can shift multiple times in that window.

Even in a down market, people are having children. They need more space. They need bedrooms. They need yards. Sometimes they need their very first house. That demand doesn't pause because headlines are negative. Even at the lowest lows of the last downturn, I still had clients with new babies buying a home for their newly expanded family. When you need a place to live, you need a place to live.

Job changes are constant as well.

Some are positive. Some are negative. Some require relocation. Some create opportunity. People sell because they're leaving, and people buy because they're arriving. This is happening all the time, in every type of market.

Marriage fits into this category too.

When people decide to get married, they're not checking market charts. They're building a life together. And often that means buying a home. That happens in strong markets and weak ones alike.

So when you zoom out, the pattern becomes obvious.

There are always reasons people need to buy and sell houses, in the best of times and in the worst of times. The only thing that really changes between an up market and a down market is how many agents are willing to keep showing up.

I live in Los Angeles. Even in a down market, there are still thousands of transactions happening every single month. You don't need all of them. You don't need hundreds of them. You need one or two.

Out of thousands, you couldn't find one or two?

That's the real question.

So the takeaway is simple: keep your head up.

Yes, there will be slow periods. Yes, the news will make it sound like the world is ending. Friends, family, and other agents will say no one is buying and no one is selling. They'll tell you to wait it out.

That story gets told in every downturn, and it's never true.

Even in the worst markets in history, transactions still happen. You only need a small percentage of them to live well. Some agents even prefer down markets because the competition thins out. While others panic or sit on the sidelines, they quietly go to work and build momentum.

I'll often challenge agents who complain about slow months. I'll say, "There were still thousands of transactions last month. You only needed one or two to make your paycheck. You couldn't get one or two?"

That question usually changes the tone of the conversation.

This is also why I don't spend much time consuming negative news. Not because I don't want to be informed, but because I don't need constant reminders that things are difficult. The market is what it is, and everyone is facing the same conditions.

My competitor down the street doesn't have a different market than I do. We're all operating in the same environment. The difference is who keeps working when it gets uncomfortable.

You don't need the market to improve.

You need to get up, go out there, and take your piece of the pie.

Keep in mind that when you're dealing with sensitive situations, especially something like an estate sale, you need to be very careful about what you say.

When my mother passed away, I was very torn about what to do with her house. Part of me thought I should move in and live there. Another part of me knew I didn't really want that. After a lot of debate, my wife and I decided we would be better off selling the house.

The problem was that the house was in San Francisco, and all of my real estate contacts were in Los Angeles. I didn't really know who to call. So I reached out to an L.A. agent I trusted and asked if they could connect me with someone in San Francisco.

Eventually, a friend of a friend of a friend came recommended.

Because I was deep in the grieving process, I didn't even think to interview anyone else. I didn't shop around. I didn't compare agents. I just signed the paperwork and listed my mom's house with him.

The process went okay overall. There were a few hiccups, but for the most part, he guided me to an offer that looked solid and likely to close.

There had actually been one offer that was slightly higher than the one we accepted, but it was 100 percent financing with no money down. In other words, there was a real risk that the deal wouldn't make it through escrow. So instead, we chose the second-highest offer from a buyer who actually had a down payment and some money in the game.

That part made sense. It made me think he was approaching this clearly.

But then there were little things along the way.

For example, I had mentioned that my mom had a lot of paint, paint thinner, and other household chemicals in the garage, items that couldn't just be tossed in the regular trash.

He told me, "Oh, I'll take care of that."

So I was a little surprised when I reviewed the final escrow statement and saw a charge for a junk removal service to clean out the garage. Apparently, his son owned the junk removal company.

Now maybe I misunderstood him. Maybe in my grief, I heard what I wanted to hear. When he said he would "take care of it," I thought he literally meant he would handle it. Instead, he hired his own son, paid him, and passed the bill along to me.

I was annoyed, but I was willing to let that go.

There was also a small issue with property taxes. Because I inherited the home, I was actually eligible to inherit my mother's property tax rate. But he didn't advise me about that, and I didn't really understand the paperwork the city sent me while the property was in my name between the time she passed and when the house sold.

That mistake ended up costing me about $500 in property taxes for the short period I owned the house.

Again, I was willing to forgive it. Maybe he didn't know. Maybe it just slipped through the cracks.

But the moment that stuck with me happened when he called to tell me the house had closed.

"The deal closed," he said. "The money is on its way. Congratulations."

Congratulations.

That word hit me like a punch in the gut.

My mother had just died. I didn't want to sell her house. I didn't want this money. What I wanted was my mom back. I wanted her to be alive and healthy.

Now, logically, I know he probably didn't mean anything by it. "Congratulations" is just something people say when a real estate transaction closes. It's almost automatic.

But in that moment, it was the wrong thing to say.

And it stuck with me.

Years later, I still remember that feeling. I never recommended him to anyone. In fact, I don't even remember his name anymore.

A few years later, I discovered that someone I went to high school with had become a very successful real estate agent in that exact area of San Francisco. If I had known that at the time, I would have hired her without hesitation. All these years later, I still wish I had hired her. She would have been more sensitive to the situation.

Instead, I ended up with someone who simply didn't read the room.

If you want referrals in this business, that matters.

Pay attention to the moment. Pay attention to the person you're talking to. And understand that sometimes the words you use, especially in sensitive situations, can determine whether someone recommends you for years, or never thinks of you again.

CHAPTER 10

Budget Like a Business Owner

The Agent's Budget Paradox

Real estate agents love to discuss budgeting with their clients as a way to save for a down payment and manage the expenses that come with buying a home. Yet many agents themselves are not great at budgeting their own money. The most successful agents, however, work from a budget.

There's a cliché about agents: after closing their first deal, they immediately lease a white Mercedes or a similar car. The idea is that the car will signal success to others, even if they're not truly successful yet. The downside may seem obvious from the outside, but it's often not obvious when you're in the middle of it. The two main issues are covering basic living expenses, rent or mortgage, food, and having enough money left for marketing.

The Irregular Income Challenge and the Pitfalls of Financial Desperation

While an agent's commission check can be large, the reality is that those checks don't come regularly. If an agent starts feeling pressure from piling bills and focuses only on the next commission, this is where problems begin.

Not necessarily with paying bills, but with putting the need for a commission ahead of their ethics and fiduciary duty to clients.

Agents who feel in desperate need of their next commission check are the agents who give other agents a bad name. These are the agents who encourage their clients not to read their home inspection report or downplay the findings. These are the agents who don't fully disclose what they know about a property or misrepresent a property's true value, or simply use high-pressure sales tactics to force their clients to make a decision they don't feel comfortable with. Such agents usually get into trouble later with unhappy clients and don't get future referrals.

By having a budget and planning out expenses in advance, an agent can feel reasonably comfortable going long periods between commission checks. Avoiding the temptation to spend commission checks quickly will help an agent greatly during slow times in the market.

The other aspect of budgeting that is important is knowing how much money an agent should spend on marketing. Some marketing tactics can be expensive, such as a billboard, while others may not cost much money but can be time-consuming, such as door knocking. Regardless, you will have marketing expenses. Business cards, brochures, flyers, and open house signs are items an agent will need to purchase. In addition, agents have MLS fees, memberships to professional organizations, phone bills, and perhaps office fees. Some of these things will have to be paid for before earning a single sale. A rookie real estate agent needs to budget what they have to get started. If you don't have a few of the basics purchased up front, you may never earn that first commission check.

How much of your commission check should be spent on marketing?

A good rule of thumb is that approximately 10 percent of gross revenue should go toward marketing. I know some aggressive agents will spend closer to 20 percent. The key is to let your revenue, commission checks, drive your marketing budget. The other key is to always set aside some of your commission for marketing. If you don't have a marketing budget or spend that money elsewhere, it can spell disaster for your real estate career.

As to how to budget

I highly recommend checking out books by Dave Ramsey for details. But here are the basics:

Calculate a Baseline Budget:

Start by determining your essential monthly expenses, including rent or mortgage, utilities, groceries, insurance, and debt payments. This forms the baseline for your budget. You must know the bare minimum it costs you to stay alive with a roof over your head.

Next, try to project your income over the next year. Keep in mind, it may take months between commission checks. Most agents only do zero to three deals a year in their first few years in the business. By planning out when you think you might earn your first few checks, you also set a goal for you to focus on.

Marketing fund: Ideally, 10 percent of your revenue should be going to marketing. Though you may have to lower that figure in lean times, and you may want to raise it when possible to be aggressive.

Establish an emergency fund. Conventional wisdom says this fund should be three to six months' worth of living expenses. This fund provides a financial safety net during lean periods. But given you may not see your next check for three to six months, setting aside an emergency fund is very difficult when starting out. It can seem impossible to find money to set aside for several years. Most people simply don't have one. Yet as impossible as this sounds, don't skip it entirely. It is a good idea to have a separate savings account where you can put aside 2 percent of your gross revenue in an emergency fund. The key is that it's an emergency fund for actual emergencies. Needing to attend your friend's bachelor or bachelorette party in Vegas is not an emergency.

Flexible Spending: Be flexible with non-essential expenses. During months with higher income, you can allocate more funds to discretionary spending, such as dinners out. Conversely, tighten your belt during lower-income months.

Expense Tracking: Keep meticulous records of your income and expenses. Tools like budgeting apps can help you monitor your financial health and make necessary adjustments. Once you get to a certain level of regular income, you might consider hiring a bookkeeper.

Regularly review your budget and adjust as needed. If you consistently earn more than expected, consider increasing your emergency fund or savings contributions.

Tax Planning

The worst part of being a 1099 independent contractor or self-employed person is that no one takes out your taxes for you. Getting a sizable tax bill at the end of the year can be quite a shock. It's not uncommon to realize you have spent the money elsewhere that you owe in taxes and now must work extra hard to earn more money to pay those taxes, which will result in more tax bills. Consult with a tax professional well before taxes are due to optimize your tax strategy. Irregular income can have tax implications, and proper planning can help you manage tax obligations efficiently. Quite simply, you need to have a good CPA to help you with taxes. I do not recommend trying to do your taxes yourself.

Seek Financial Advice

If budgeting with irregular income proves challenging, consider consulting a financial advisor who specializes in variable income scenarios. They can provide tailored guidance to suit your situation.

Chapter 11

Follow-Up Like You Mean It

There's an old saying in business:

"The fortune is in the follow-up."

And it's true, especially in real estate.

Most agents think that means following up with new leads.

But the real pros? They know it also means following up with past clients.

So let's break this down into two parts:

Following up with leads
Following up with past clients

Part 1: Following Up with Leads (and Not Blowing It)

If you're door knocking, cold calling, running ads, working open houses, or however you're generating leads, eventually someone's going to say:

"Not right now… but maybe in 30 days."

Well, guess what?

That means you follow up in 30 days.

Not 31. Not when you feel like it. Thirty. Exactly.

Because one extra day could be the difference between you and the next agent who knocks on their door or calls first. Timing matters. People move fast. If you're not organized, you lose.

I know an agent who makes 50 phone calls a day, to past clients, friends, warm leads, and even people he met once at a wedding. And to do that, he's got to stay organized. He keeps a handwritten list with a pencil, no fancy CRM, but he tracks who he's called and who's up next. Every day.

So how do you stay organized?

That's up to you.

There is no "right" way. There's only your way.

I see agents argue online about which CRM is best. The best software is not the real question. The best CRM is the one you'll actually use. It may be as simple as a Google Sheet, a dry-erase board, or a dozen sticky notes slapped onto your bathroom mirror. Or it might be as complex as a full sales software system. The question is which system will you actually use every day, and which system will you set up and never use again?

That's the point: Your system doesn't have to impress anyone else. It just has to work for you.

People Love When You Remember Their Name

Write it down. Every time.

Because people notice when you remember them.

And they notice even more when you don't.

I'm always surprised when agents call my inspection company and say, "Hey, I need to book an inspection for a client..."

And when we ask, "What's the client's name?"

They go, "Uhhh… good question."

How are you in escrow and you can't remember your client's name?!

That's wild to me. But it happens more than you think.

So take notes. Keep records. Make the effort to remember who people are, because that tiny detail might be the reason someone chooses to work with you again, or decides not to.

Meet People Where They Are (Communication Matters)

This one's easy to mess up:

If someone texts you, text them back.
If they email you, email them back.
If they call, call them back.

Don't be the person who responds to an email with a phone call, or replies to a text with a five-paragraph email. People have their preferred method of communication, so use it and respect it.

Want to earn someone's trust? Start by showing them you're paying attention.

Part 2: Following Up with Past Clients (and Why They Forget You)

Here's the truth nobody likes to admit:

A lot of clients don't use the same agent for their next transaction.

And the reason?

They straight-up forgot who their agent was.

Yep. The National Association of Realtors has published studies after study that show most buyers and sellers don't remember their agent years later.

Some of that is due to industry churn. But the biggest reason?

The agent never stayed in touch.

You're going to be different.

Whether it's a postcard, an email, a birthday card, or a funny Thanksgiving mailer, you need some kind of system to stay top-of-mind.

You want your clients to remember:

That you're a real estate agent

That you work on commission, not a salary

That you're still available when they're ready again

Because if you don't remind them, someone else will.

A Story About Staying in the Picture

The agent who helped my wife and me buy both of our homes?

They were friends of a friend, actually the parents of one of our friends.

They invited us over. Stayed in touch.

And when it came time to buy again, they were the natural choice.

Why? Because they stayed in our lives.

Contrast that with the lender we used for the first house.

He barely listened. He didn't build rapport.

By the time we closed, I couldn't wait to be done with him.

Guess who didn't get our second loan?

See the difference?

Relationships matter. Staying connected matters.

I'm not saying you need to be besties with every past client, but they should never wonder if you're still in the business.

Some Clients Remember Us, But Not Their Agent

At my inspection company, we occasionally get a call from someone saying,

"Hey, you guys did our inspection a few years ago, we're moving, and we want to use you again!"

We'll ask, "Are you still working with the same real estate agent?"

And they'll say, "No, why would we be?"

That says a lot.

We were just the inspectors.

But we stayed in their memory because we stayed professional, friendly, and helpful.

If your clients remember your inspector and not you, something went wrong.

You have to earn that loyalty. Stay in their world.

How to Stay Connected Without Being Annoying

Refer back to the earlier marketing chapters, but here's the shortlist:

Add every client to your social media

Send occasional check-ins, updates, or just-for-fun messages

Mail something real, like birthday cards, holiday cards, etc.

Choose holidays people don't expect, like Thanksgiving or Halloween

Share tips, reminders, or local news once in a while

Just don't make it all about you.

If people feel like you're only checking in when you want something, they'll tune you out.

But if you show real interest in their life, their family, their journey, they'll remember you when it matters.

Bottom Line: The Agents Who Stay in Touch Win

It's not about having the most high-tech CRM.

It's about building the habit of following up, with new leads, with old clients, with people who could refer you tomorrow.

You're not just planting seeds. You're tending the garden.

Because in this business, people forget fast.

But if you stay consistent, present, and intentional, they'll remember the one who didn't forget them.

Every agent claims they want to be "Your Lifetime agent," but very few act as if they mean it.

Mark was a semi-successful real estate agent. He had been in the business for 10 years. He wasn't living a luxury life. He wasn't closing tons of deals, but he closed enough every year to make a decent living. He couldn't complain, but he'd certainly like to do more.

One day, he was in a coffee shop when he spotted Stephen and Carol across the room. Stephen and Carol had been his clients many years ago. He had been introduced to them through a friend of a friend and guided them through their first home purchase.

Mark thought to himself, "Wow, I haven't seen them in a long time. When was the last time I talked to them? Well, let's see here."

He thought, "I remember I sent them a holiday card in December after closing, and I sent them a calendar that one year I decided to do calendars. I haven't talked to them since, I don't remember."

Regardless, Mark still considered them his clients. And it had been a few years, so maybe they were thinking about selling? Mark was getting itchy about when his next deal would be, and the sale and purchase of a bigger home would help his bank account right about now.

Mark went up to them and said hi. Stephen and Carol got big smiles on their faces. They were obviously very happy to see Mark.

"Hi, how are you doing?" they said. "It's great to see you."

They started chatting, mostly small talk at first. Finally, Mark got up the courage to ask the big question:

"So, how is that house working out for you?"

"Oh," Stephen replied. "Well, we sold it and bought another house last year."

Stephen continued talking, without realizing the dagger he was pushing into Mark's thoughts.

"You know, Carol and I were talking about maybe we should find something bigger, and we just happened to drive by an open house sign. So, on a whim, we stopped in, and we fell in love with the place. The listing agent had a sales contract right there, so we just signed it."

Ouch, Mark thought. It was bad enough he lost the deal, but to think they went unrepresented by an agent of their own and just let the other agent double-end the deal really stung.

Carol went on, "We were thinking of keeping the first house as a rental, but there was an agent who lives down the street from us, who knocks on our door here and there. And when he showed us how much we could get for our house, we just went with it."

Double ouch. Not only did he lose this deal, but he got upstaged by a less experienced agent who door-knocked clients he thought were his.

Mark tried to hide the disappointment on his face, but Stephen and Carol could tell something was off.

Carol spoke up. "Look, it was nothing personal. We just weren't really thinking about it that way."

Stephen nodded and added, "Yeah, and besides, you've been with your company for a long time. I'm sure they take good care of you."

Triple ouch.

That sentence hit Mark harder than anything else they had said.

They didn't say it to be cruel. In fact, they looked a little uncomfortable telling Mark the story. But the message was clear.

They hadn't meant to replace him.

They hadn't simply forgotten about him.

It was much worse than being forgotten. Stephen and Carol thought it didn't matter.

They thought Mark had a salary.

They assumed he worked for a company that paid him a lump sum every few weeks. In their minds, whether Mark sold a house or not probably didn't matter much. If he happened to close a deal, great, maybe he'd get a little bonus or something. But otherwise, surely the company "took care of him."

They had no idea that real estate agents are almost always 100 percent commission-based.

They didn't realize that when they bought that house years ago, Mark didn't get a paycheck unless the deal closed. They didn't realize that helping them buy and sell homes was literally how he made his living. If he didn't close deals, he didn't get paid. Period.

But why would they know that?

Mark had never explained it.

Mark finished the conversation politely. They chatted a bit more, wished each other well, and eventually went their separate ways. But as Mark walked back to his car, he couldn't stop replaying the conversation in his head.

Not only had he failed to stay in contact with them over the years, not only had he allowed himself to drift completely out of their lives, but they didn't even understand how real estate worked.

He had never stayed in touch with them. He hadn't added them on social media. He hadn't checked in once a year. He hadn't dropped by with a second calendar or a quick "how's the house treating you?" message. It would have taken five seconds to add them to his social media feed. Yet, he hadn't.

Years had passed, and in that time, Mark had quietly faded into the background of their lives. He had failed at being the Chief Repeating Officer.

So when the moment came to buy another house, they walked into the first open house they saw.

And when it was time to sell, they signed with the agent who had been knocking on their door.

The truth slowly settled in as Mark walked back to his car. His mind kept racing with the reality that he had lost two commissions over not keeping in touch.

And the most painful part, Mark knew deep down it wasn't really Stephen and Carol's fault that they didn't call him.

It was his.

CHAPTER 12

Build Your Tribe

They say it takes a village to raise a child. In real estate, it takes a village to close a house.

You may be the point guard. You're the face of the transaction. The strategist. The one setting expectations and managing emotion. But behind every smooth closing is a network of professionals who make you look good.

If you want to build a long-term career, you need to build your tribe.

Start with lenders.

It doesn't matter how skilled you are at negotiating contracts if your client can't qualify for the loan. No loan, no sale. The smartest agents don't rely on just one lender. They build relationships with two or three who complement each other. One who thrives with first-time buyers and hand-holding. Another who understands jumbo loans and complex financial structures. Maybe a third who knows how to solve the oddball situations, unconventional properties, self-employed borrowers, layered income scenarios.

And here's something most agents overlook: your client may talk to the lender as much as they talk to you, sometimes more. If the lender is slow to respond, confusing, or dismissive, that frustration reflects back on you. Choose people who answer the phone. Choose people you enjoy talking to. Choose people who elevate your client's experience.

Next is escrow.

As you move closer to closing, your escrow officer becomes one of your most important allies. Are the documents in? What conditions remain? Is there a last-minute issue with wiring instructions or a payoff demand?

A good escrow officer is worth their weight in gold. A great one feels like a teammate. You'll be in frequent communication, often under time pressure. You want someone calm, organized, and solution-oriented, not someone who disappears when things get tense.

You're also going to want a strong relationship with at least one insurance agent, ideally more than one.

Insurance has become increasingly complicated, particularly in California. I've personally seen deals fall apart at the last minute because a buyer couldn't secure coverage. Not because they lacked funds. Not because the loan fell through. But because the property itself created underwriting issues they didn't anticipate.

Fire zones. Floodplains. Hillside construction. Older roofs. Knob-and-tube wiring. Each property has characteristics that may make insurance easy, or very difficult to obtain.

A few years ago, California even modified the residential purchase contract to separate insurance into its own contingency, distinct from the loan and inspection contingencies. That change alone should tell you how serious the issue has become.

You should have a go-to insurance professional for clients who don't already have one. And you should have a backup, sometimes even a third option. Not every broker has access to every carrier. Not every carrier will write every risk.

When insurance becomes an obstacle, you don't want to be scrambling. You want to be making a call.

Then there's title.

Title insurance doesn't get much attention when things are clean. But when something strange shows up on a preliminary report, an easement from a local utility company is common. Perhaps a neighbor has an easement over a partially shared driveway. A prior owner may have an heir who somehow still has a legal claim to the property. That's when your relationship with your title rep matters.

These issues must be resolved before closing. Your job isn't to be a title attorney. Your job is to understand enough to guide your client confidently and to have someone you trust when you need clarification. A strong title rep makes complicated situations feel manageable.

And then we come to the home inspector.

Some agents are tempted to choose an inspector who won't "rock the boat." That's short-term thinking. Every real estate attorney will tell you the same thing: most lawsuits stem from lack of disclosure. Someone knew, or reasonably should have known, something and didn't say it.

You are far better off having everything disclosed up front. A thorough inspection might make a buyer nervous in the moment, but it protects everyone long term. Deals fall apart. Lawsuits because someone didn't disclose or find a problem haunt careers. Choose inspectors who are fair, impartial, and detailed. Choose people who document well. Choose professionals you'd want inspecting your own home.

Some agents next want a transaction coordinator. A transaction coordinator may be independent or someone who works for your brokerage. Eventually, you may even hire your own personal TC. They keep track of the stacks of paperwork necessary to complete a transaction. They ensure the right forms are signed, deadlines are met, and they keep communication going until closing. A good TC is often worth their weight in gold.

Another relationship you should cultivate is with a real estate attorney.

And I emphasize real estate attorney.

This is not your general business attorney. Not a criminal defense attorney. Not a divorce attorney. Real estate law is its own discipline.

You may need one when a boundary dispute arises over a fence or a tree on the property line. You may need one when a tenant situation becomes complicated. You may need one if a past client claims you failed to disclose something and legal defense becomes necessary.

In previous chapters, we discussed how most real estate lawsuits stem from disclosure issues. When something escalates beyond a simple conversation, you want someone in your corner who understands the contracts, the timelines, and the standard of care in your industry.

Even if you never need to use them, having a trusted real estate attorney in your back pocket provides confidence. And sometimes confidence alone changes how you handle a situation.

If you're representing sellers, you'll also want strong staging relationships.

As a buyer's agent, staging isn't central to your daily work. As a listing agent, it can dramatically impact price and speed.

There are generally two types of stagers.

The first is what most people picture: a company with a warehouse full of furniture. They bring in curated pieces, art, and décor to transform a vacant property into something aspirational.

The second type works with what your client already owns. They rearrange, declutter, refine, and elevate existing furniture so the home shows in its best possible light while the seller is still living there.

Some stagers do both. Regardless, having the right one for the right situation can add tangible value to a listing.

As your business grows and you begin working with higher-net-worth clients or investors, you'll also benefit from knowing a strong CPA or tax strategist.

Capital gains questions. Investment properties. Rental income. Commercial transactions. 1031 exchanges. These are not areas where you should be improvising advice.

When a client asks a tax-related question, the most powerful answer you can give is, "Let me connect you with someone who specializes in that."

It reinforces that you understand the limits of your role, and that you're surrounded by professionals who can handle what you don't.

Beyond the obvious transaction players, your value grows with every reliable name you can confidently share. The more people you know, the more valuable your clients will see in you.

Movers are one aspect that most agents overlook. But every seller needs to move out, and every buyer needs to move in. Most agents leave this to chance, letting their clients find their own. But if you have worked so hard to have a clean sales process, do you really want the last piece of the process to go haywire?

And then painters. Sellers often want or need to paint to make their house show well. Buyers often want to paint to customize their home to their tastes. Do you know a good painter who can do a good job on a tight deadline?

Every home inspection will find an issue (more on that in the next chapter). Do you know a good contractor? An electrician? A plumber?

What about other services your clients may need? Dog walker? House cleaner? A great local pizza place?

The more names you know, the more names know you.

And that resource list should be curated, not random.

Don't recommend someone just because you have a business card. Recommend people you've worked with, or who have proven themselves through people you trust. And if someone drops the ball, remove them. Your credibility is tied to every name you give out.

Your list may never be finished. However, you're always meeting new professionals. Every transaction expands your network.

Here's the part most agents miss: your clients are part of your tribe too.

Pay attention to what they do for a living. The buyer who installs driveways may become the solution for a future listing with cracked concrete. The client who runs an aquarium service might be exactly who you need next year when another client panics over a leaking custom tank. The CPA, the roofer, the landscape architect, every client expands your ecosystem.

Over time, your tribe becomes a living, breathing network. Not a spreadsheet of vendors. A community of people who trust you and whom you trust in return.

And that's when things start to change.

You stop being just another agent trying to get to the next closing. You become the connector. The problem solver. The hub.

That's hard to replace.

At some point in your career, you stop chasing every deal and you start living off referrals. Referrals from past clients. Referrals from their friends and family. Referrals from professionals you've worked alongside for years.

And here's the interesting part: it will rarely be equal.

You may send dozens of clients to your home inspector over the course of a year. That inspector may never send you a single deal back. The lender might refer you occasionally. The escrow officer probably won't. The painter and the plumber almost certainly won't.

That's not the point.

You don't build your network to keep score. You build it because it elevates your client's experience, and that's what ultimately drives referrals back to you.

Think about it from the client's perspective.

If they liked you, but the lender you recommended was unresponsive...

If they liked you, but the inspector felt rushed or dismissive…

If they liked you, but escrow was chaotic…

Their memory of the transaction becomes mixed. They may still recommend you, but without enthusiasm.

Now imagine the opposite.

The lender was proactive.

The inspector was thorough and professional.

Escrow was smooth and organized.

The contractor showed up on time.

The mover made a stressful day easy.

When every piece of the process feels coordinated and professional, the client walks away thinking, "That was a great experience."

And who gets the credit?

You do.

That's when referrals multiply. That's when friends and family hear, "You have to call my agent." Not a lukewarm recommendation, but a confident one.

You attract far more people with honey than vinegar. A strong network creates honey. It makes you look prepared, connected, and capable in almost any situation.

Over time, your tribe becomes your competitive advantage.

CHAPTER 13

Manage Expectations

The biggest difference I see between top agents and average agents isn't charisma. It isn't marketing. It isn't even negotiation skills.

It's expectation management.

When expectations aren't set, clients fill in the blanks with fantasy.

They start asking themselves:

How much should we really pay for this house?
Should we still buy this house?
Do we even want this house anymore?

Confusion turns into anxiety. Anxiety turns into doubt. Doubt turns into emotional decisions.

I've seen buyers cry at the end of an inspection because the house they "fell in love with" suddenly feels flawed. The house didn't change. Their expectations did.

Your job is to manage expectations at every step of the transaction.

Not just the fun parts.

Every step.

Let's start with the loan process.

You don't have to be a loan officer. But you should understand how loans actually work. The best agents I know can explain mortgage programs clearly, even if they aren't originating the loan themselves. They know what "pre-approval" really means. They know that approval almost always comes with conditions. They know that underwriting will ask for more paperwork, sometimes at the last minute.

Most buyers think pre-approval equals a done deal. It doesn't. It means, "Based on what we see so far, we think this could work."

If you don't explain that upfront, your client feels blindsided when underwriting asks for more documents. They feel buried. Overwhelmed. Frustrated.

One of the most successful agents I've ever met really knows her loan programs. What sets her apart is that when she meets somebody, she has answers to questions. You will find, typically, when a real estate agent meets someone randomly, that person says, "Oh, *I'd love to buy a house someday. But I could never afford it.*" Or *"I don't have the money. I'm not in a place in my life to buy a house right now.*" Yet this agent, because she knows all her loan programs and all the first-time buyer programs, and every possible little grant out there, can easily take someone who says they can't afford it and quickly show them that, yes, they actually could buy a house. I've seen it many times where someone who thought they would never be able to buy a house is, 30 days later, holding the keys to their first place. Now, she's not a loan officer. She's not doing the loan officer's job for them, but she knows all the programs, and it gives her a huge advantage over other agents who would simply say, *"Oh, well, let's keep in touch in case you ever decide."*

Now let's talk about title insurance.

I remember buying my first house and seeing the charge at closing. I was irritated. I didn't remember agreeing to it. I didn't understand what it was. I even got a little mad at my agent.

"You need it, you have to have it," he said.

That was the explanation.

Even the second time around, I still felt annoyed seeing that line item. It wasn't until years later, after interviewing a title rep on my podcast, that I actually understood what I was paying for and why it mattered. It should have been explained to me well before I got to the closing table.

The same principle applies to inspections.

Inspections create more anxiety than almost any other part of the transaction.

You don't need to be a home inspector. In fact, you shouldn't pretend to be one. But you absolutely should explain what the inspection is, and what it isn't.

An inspection looks at safety and function. It is not a crystal ball. It is not destructive testing like you see on TV. Inspectors don't know what's behind walls. They aren't there to tell your client whether to buy the house. They are there to document facts.

No house is perfect. There will always be findings. Always. Even a brand-new house can have issues. In fact, some brand-new houses I have inspected were worse than a typical used home. Regardless, I have never walked out of any home without reporting on something.

If your client walks into an inspection expecting a clean report, you failed to prepare them.

In California, the residential purchase contract even outlines how the inspection process works. It encourages buyer attendance. The California Association of Realtors reinforces this in its materials. None of this should be a surprise.

One of the clearest signs that expectations weren't set?

When a buyer asks the inspector mid-inspection, "Who pays for that?"

That question means the inspection process was not explained up front, that it's the inspector's job to document the condition of the property and that there will be a list of issues that can be addressed by you, the agent.

After the report comes out, the standard options for the buyer are:

The buyer can accept the property as-is.
The buyer can cancel within their contingency period.
The buyer can request repairs or negotiate credits.

And the seller has three basic responses:

Yes.
Partially.
No.

That's it.

But when clients don't understand those lanes ahead of time, they start distrusting the process. They think the inspector "found too much." They ask for unrealistic discounts. They panic over normal maintenance items. Or they walk away from a good house because they weren't thinking clearly.

Bad agents wait until after the inspection and then manage the meltdown.

Good agents explain upfront: "The inspector is going to find things. That's their job. Once we see the full picture, we'll decide how to respond."

A case in point, I was once inspecting a true fixer-upper in an otherwise good neighborhood. The house had a lot of issues. As I was going, the buyer kept a running tab in her head of how much it would cost to fix everything. At the end of the inspection, she felt she would be able to negotiate that entire cost off the asking price. The issue was that the house had been heavily pre-discounted below market value by the sellers because they were aware that the house needed substantial repairs. The agent was now in a bind because their buyer expected a dollar-for-dollar reduction in price, when the agent knew that many of these costs were already baked into the asking price, and expecting another significant reduction was not realistic. This created a very uncomfortable conversation that almost ruined the deal. All of this could have been avoided by having a conversation up front.

Another common mistake I see is agents reacting mid-inspection. The inspector mentions an issue, and the agent goes into crisis mode.

"Who can fix that?"

"I know a contractor."

"Let's call someone right now."

Slow down.

Let the inspection finish.

You don't even know if that issue will matter in the bigger picture. By the time the inspection is complete, that "big problem" might not even be in the top five concerns. Or it may be small compared to something else. Or the buyer may decide they don't want the house for an entirely different reason.

Don't solve a problem before you understand the scope of the problem.

Now, back to loans for a moment.

Most buyers have no idea how document-heavy the loan process is. They don't realize that a pre-approval is not the same as an approval. An approval usually comes with a variety of conditions that have to be met before the loan can be fully approved. They don't realize that underwriters can ask for updated bank statements, letters of explanation, verification of employment, and many other documents. And what really blows people's minds is that even after the loan has closed, the lender has the right to reach out and ask for additional documents. I used to work in the post-closing department of a lender, and I often had to verify facts weeks, if not months, after the loan and the home had closed.

If you don't set that expectation, your client feels like the lender is incompetent or the deal is falling apart.

Your job is to say early on:

"This process will feel repetitive. It will be long. They may ask for more paperwork, and they may ask more than once. This is entirely normal."

That sentence alone can prevent weeks of stress.

But here's the balance.

As much as you want to prepare clients for friction, you don't want to scare them.

Expectation management is not pessimism.

It's confidence.

You're not saying, "This will be a disaster."

You're saying, "Here's how this works. Here's what's normal. Here's what we do if X happens."

When clients know what's coming next, they relax. They feel guided. They feel represented.

And that's the real difference.

Successful agents don't just open doors and write offers.

They reduce emotional volatility. They remove surprises. They create clarity in a process that often feels chaotic.

As much as you need to set expectations, you also have to stay in your lane.

I've seen agents try to control every single moving part of a transaction. They want to choose the lender, micromanage the lender's paperwork, pick the inspector, tell the inspector what to look at, tell the inspector what not to look at, decide what "should" be in the report, and then they wonder why everyone involved is frustrated.

You're a real estate agent. You're not the loan officer, the underwriter, the title officer, the inspector, the roofer, the electrician, or the project manager.

If you try to be all of those roles, you'll drive the professionals nuts, you'll confuse the buyer, and you'll create liability you never needed.

But the opposite extreme is just as bad.

Some agents act completely blasé about the process. They don't have relationships with lenders. They don't know inspectors. They don't have a title contact they trust. They basically toss the buyer into the deep end and say, "Good luck, text me when you need me."

That's not guidance. That's avoidance.

And it's a problem because buyers aren't paying you to open doors and fill out paperwork. They're paying you to navigate the maze. They're paying you to explain what happens next. They're paying you to keep the process moving while helping them stay calm and make good decisions.

So what does "staying in your lane" actually mean?

It means you don't do other people's jobs, but you do know enough to explain the flow.

You don't have to underwrite the loan, but you should be able to explain the loan timeline, why conditions happen, and what "normal" feels like.

You don't have to be a home inspector, but you should be able to explain what the inspection is for, how findings are reported, and what choices the buyer has afterward.

You don't have to be a title officer, but you should be able to explain why title matters and what the buyer is paying for before they see the numbers at the closing table and feel blindsided.

Your job is to guide the client from "We like this house" to the closing table without surprises, confusion, or emotional whiplash.

Staying in your lane does not mean staying shallow.

It means respecting professional boundaries while being deeply informed about how the entire process works.

If you don't understand financing at all, you'll miss opportunities for your clients. If you try to control financing, you'll create friction.

The sweet spot is this: know enough to open doors for your clients, not just the front door of the house, but the door to the possibility of ownership.

That's leadership.

And leadership is what clients are actually paying for.

CHAPTER 14

Keep Your Eye on the Big Picture: Stories from the Field

The difference between average agents and great agents isn't knowledge. It isn't charisma. It isn't even negotiation skills.

It's perspective.

Average agents react to what's directly in front of them. A bad inspection report. An emotional client. A screaming listing agent. A deal that falls apart. They see the immediate problem and assume that's the whole story.

Great agents pause. They zoom out. They ask what's really going on.

Because in real estate, the house is almost never the real issue.

Over the years, I've seen this play out again and again.

One day, I showed up to inspect a condo in Santa Clarita. I briefly met the buyers, a nice couple with five kids. Five kids, two-bedroom condo. That alone caught my attention. They left with the children, and I began the inspection.

Almost immediately, things started going wrong. I flipped a bathroom light switch, and sparks flew from the electrical panel located in a bedroom. When I tried to turn on the air conditioning, the lights dimmed throughout the unit. There were major electrical concerns and clear safety issues.

I kept thinking about those kids. Where would they sleep? How could they safely live here? I pulled the agent aside and said, "I don't think you can ethically sell this to them."

She looked at me calmly and said, "You don't understand their story. If this doesn't close in thirty days, they'll be sleeping in their car. Everybody has to live somewhere."

That sentence stopped me.

Everybody has to live somewhere. It wasn't my job to decide whether the home was ideal. My job was to explain the conditions clearly and let them choose. The agent understood the bigger picture. She wasn't ignoring the problems, she was weighing them against reality. In the bigger picture, safety issues can be fixed. Bunk beds can be arranged. Not having a place to live is a much more important issue. I should have known. I've traveled to third-world countries. I have seen entire families living in one-room huts. This condo was a luxury home by comparison to things I have seen.

Another time, I was inspecting a kitchen with a large crack running across the countertop and a cabinet pulling away from the ceiling. In my mind, it was a fixer-upper with issues.

The buyer walked in, hugged the countertop, and said she loved the kitchen and wouldn't change a thing. I kept my thoughts to myself, but I couldn't help but wonder. Love the big crack in the tile? Love a cabinet that is barely hanging on by the end of a nail? But her enthusiasm was genuine.

Because the agent was Mary, whom I spoke about earlier, we have a good relationship. So I asked her about it. Mary explained that the buyer had lived her entire life in a mobile home park. This was not only the first house she would own, but the first house she would ever live in with a solid foundation. To her, that kitchen was perfect, not because it was flawless, but because it was hers.

Soon after that experience, I inspected a luxury home in a high-end neighborhood. Beautiful kitchen. Impeccable finishes. I actually said to the buyer, “What a great kitchen!” The buyer casually told me they were going to tear it out and move it to another room because his wife didn’t like it.

Same city. Same profession. Completely different perspectives.

It wasn’t my story. It wasn’t my money. It wasn’t my life.

Every buyer has a story. Agents who understand that story serve their clients better. Agents who ignore it struggle.

I learned a similar lesson long before real estate.

When I worked at a musical instrument store, a scruffy man walked in wearing worn clothes and an old jacket. He looked borderline homeless. The assumption spread that he was near homeless, and was not there to buy anything. It was decided that an assistant manager would escort him out of the store.

As the assistant manager approached, the man reached up to touch a guitar, revealing a very expensive watch. The watch caught the assistant manager’s eye. Why would a near-homeless man be wearing an expensive watch? Instead of escorting him out, the manager asked him some probing questions.

The man turned out to be a highly successful inventor. He was rather eccentric and unconcerned with appearance. Yet, he was fully capable of buying the most expensive guitar in the store. And his Amex card went through just fine when he picked out what he wanted.

You can't judge a book by its cover. And you can't judge a buyer by what they're wearing.

Resilience in this business often looks like a calm perspective.

I once inspected a house, and for the most part, it was going okay, what you would expect for a house of its age, until I got into the crawlspace, where I noticed a portion of the foundation concrete was deteriorating. I mentioned it to the buyer's agent, who seemed not very concerned. But he wanted me to go over everything with the listing agent. When I said the foundation had deteriorated, the listing agent began screaming at me, the buyer's agent, and anyone else around. She ranted that she had backup offers and wouldn't reduce the price one cent.

The buyer's agent didn't react. He stayed calm. He knew that the defect wouldn't disappear for the next buyer. I didn't care for being screamed at and removed myself from the situation. I hadn't driven more than a few miles when my phone rang. It was the buyer's agent. He told me the listing agent agreed to a $5,000 price reduction to go toward fixing the foundation. He had simply let her scream, and once she got it out of her system, he calmly negotiated a number both sides could live with. Most people would have done what I did and left, or screamed back, or threatened to get a real estate attorney involved. But by staying calm and focused on the bigger picture, that is, securing the house and acceptable terms for his buyer, he was able to close the deal despite the issues.

On another property, this one was perched on a hillside. On the inside, it had been extensively remodeled. New floors, new counters, a completely updated kitchen, and bathrooms. No expense was spared, until I went under the home. The wood holding up the home was mostly rotted away. Much of the wood was soft to the touch. A central post that had once been four inches thick was reduced to a mere toothpick in diameter. It was scary. One wrong move, and the whole house could topple down the hillside. Most agents would have panicked. Most buyers would have walked.

Larry was the buyer's agent for this property. Larry hadn't been an agent for long, but he had been in sales his entire professional career. He looked at the bigger picture. The seller would be on the hook for the foundation regardless of whether he kept it, sold it to someone else, or sold it to his buyer. So why not get the seller to agree to repairs for his buyer? Larry gathered two foundation repair quotes, presented them to the listing agent, and calmly explained that the issue would have to be disclosed to the next buyer anyway, and there was no way out of this situation. The foundation would need to be repaired for anyone to buy this house. After coming to terms with the reality of the situation, the seller agreed to cover approximately $25,000 in repairs. Larry closed the deal, earned his commission, and looked like the hero.

Anything can be fixed, if you're willing to deal with it rationally.

But not every story ends that way, especially when an agent loses focus on the big picture and gets caught up in the details.

I got a call from an agent named Samantha. She had been referred to me by a mutual friend. Samantha's client was buying a small condo. Nothing fancy. This condo had some electrical issues, and the oven didn't work. A few weeks later, Samantha called me again, and we inspected a second condo for the same buyer. This one also had some electrical issues and an old furnace that was no longer safe to run. A few weeks after that, Samantha and her clients had me inspect a third condo that had similar issues. Each unit had typical lower-end issues, and each time, the deal fell apart.

Eventually, Samantha told me she couldn't use me anymore because I was "killing her deals."

Except that, if you stepped back, I wasn't killing Samantha's deals. Expectations were.

The buyer's budget only allowed for fixer-uppers, and Samantha kept showing the buyer only fixer-uppers. But the buyer's parents, who were heavily involved, wanted their daughter to have something move-in ready. It was the parents who kept saying, "This isn't good enough." Samantha hadn't aligned the budget with expectations. Samantha hadn't explained that at this price point, every unit is bound to have some significant issues. The inspection report simply exposed that disconnect. Samantha didn't need a different inspector, Samantha needed a heart-to-heart conversation about the fact that, in this price range, there will be issues. And regardless, no house or condo is going to be completely free of problems. Without understanding the bigger picture, Samantha was spinning her wheels, showing units that the buyer would not buy, and not recognizing the reality of the situation.

In another case, the agent I frequently worked with, John, had me come to inspect a house for his buyers. It was a hoarder house. Piles of magazines and who knows what else stacked to the ceiling, just small pathways between piles to get from one room to the next. The kitchen hadn't been cleaned in years. I was very limited in what I could do, but the buyer understood, told me to do my best, and left. I tried my best, but most things were not visible. The listing agent was there for a while, but at some point she left, and then it was just the seller and me. I went outside to check on something and came back in, only to realize the seller wasn't aware I was still there. So I decided I needed to get out of there.

A few months later, I ran into John, and I asked him what had happened. The buyers had apparently decided to buy the house anyway, on the condition that the seller move out. But as weeks went by, the seller made no attempt to move. The seller made no attempt to clean up the property. It was eventually determined that the seller was suffering from dementia. He was mentally incapable of selling the house. The listing agent, eager to earn a sale, had ignored the evidence, put the house on the market, and accepted the buyer's offer, all while pretending not to realize the seller was in no condition to sell. It could have become a legal mess. Charges could have been filed. John was angry about how it went down, but told me, in the bigger picture, this wasn't worth the problems, and walked away from the deal.

A similar situation occurred in another transaction. I got a call from a buyer who had gotten my name from a broker I only knew by reputation. I was honored to get that recommendation, so I was eager to do the job. Upon showing up, the seller made a threat to not let her dog out or else. That should have been a red flag, but as a dog owner myself, I brushed it off. As the inspection went on, the seller became more erratic. I learned as I went along that she had recently become a widow after her husband passed very unexpectedly. In short, she did not want to sell the house. I attempted to inspect the crawlspace, and from below, I could hear her throwing a full-on temper tantrum and throwing chairs around. I quickly got myself out of there. In retrospect, the listing agent was too quick to put the house on the market. The listing agent didn't look at the big picture that this woman was not in a state of mind to sell. Perhaps she needed to get out from under the mortgage, but the timing was not right. By going too quickly, the sale was almost derailed. Months later, I found out the sale did go through, but not without its problems.

Contrast that with an older couple I once met during an inspection. The buyers were discussing remodel plans in front of them. The buyers had me there, along with contractors discussing the impending remodel. After a while, the buyer looked embarrassed. He realized he was talking about completely erasing this couple's history in the home, right in front of them. Instead of taking offense, the sellers said, "If it helps the house sell quicker, we're all for it." This listing agent had explained the big picture to the sellers, and the sellers were onboard. A conversation ahead of time had saved them from a potentially awkward situation.

Motivation changes everything.

And sometimes the bigger picture is just to realize a transaction is a dead end. I had been called by a buyer to inspect a condo. I didn't know the agent involved, but I met the buyer ahead of time to discuss the buyer's concerns. As the inspection went on, the buyer started asking more and more questions, deeply concerned by aspects that were either trivial, like window curtains, or out of my hands, like where the walls of the building were located relative to each other. A week later, the buyer called me and started screaming at me that I had missed the mold under the sink, that she had gone back with another inspector who found mold under the sink. I pulled up my report and saw there was clearly no mold in any of my photos. In fact, the areas under the sink were relatively clean. But the buyer wasn't having it; she insisted I had missed it, called me names, and hung up.

Several months later, I saw that agent at a real estate event. I really wanted to know her take. Did she think I missed it? Was she mad at me? Or did she think the buyer overreacted? I nervously approached her and brought up the story. She said calmly, "Some people just shouldn't buy a house."

She wasn't blaming me. She understood that this buyer just was not ready to commit to owning a home, and that she had walked away from the transaction, realizing that closing a deal with this buyer was not going to happen.

I have never completed an inspection without at least one item on the report. Houses require maintenance, just like cars require fuel and oil, just like our bodies require food and water.

The agents who thrive in this business understand all of this.

They understand that the house is rarely the true problem. It's expectations. It's emotional readiness. It's budget reality. It's motivation. It's fear.

Anyone can react to a defect.

Professionals interpret what the defect means in the context of the bigger picture. The best agents explain the buying and selling process upfront.

Resilience in real estate isn't about being loud or aggressive. It's about staying composed long enough to see what's actually happening in front of you.

The cracked countertop isn't the issue.

The rotted beam isn't the issue.

The inspection report isn't the issue.

The issue is perspective.

And the agents who master that, who see beyond the surface and refuse to be reactive, are the ones who can get through almost anything. The agents who overreact to an issue or a transaction going sideways often don't last long term.

When lecturing, I always say, "It's better to walk away from a transaction than get sued later." Long-term agents live on referrals, and the best way to get referrals is to give stellar customer service, not just try to close the deal because you have bills due this month.

CHAPTER 15
Track What Matters

As an agent, it's important to track what actually matters in your business.

Most agents tend to look only at the bottom line.

How many houses did I sell this year?

How much money did I make?

Those numbers matter, of course, but they only tell you the result. They don't tell you how you got there. And if you don't understand how you got there, you won't know how to get back there again.

Think of it this way: the final numbers are the finish line. But if you only stare at the finish line, you'll never understand the path that got you there. Tracking is also important because it can reveal uncomfortable truths.

It's very easy for someone to say, "I worked all day." Maybe you went into the office early, stayed nine hours, and were the last person to leave. From the outside, it feels like you worked like a rock star.

But when you look at your tracking, the story can look very different.

Maybe you made five phone calls. You sent three emails. In between, you chatted with another agent about the game, spent time at the water cooler, and took a two-hour lunch.

You came back to the office and spent a few hours scrolling social media. Maybe you read a couple of interesting articles online about history or something else that caught your attention.

Then, toward the end of the day, you sent two more emails and made another phone call.

On paper, the day looked long. It felt busy. But when you look at the numbers, the actual productive work was very small.

Tracking forces you to confront reality. It shows you the difference between being busy and being productive.

More importantly, it holds you accountable.

When you track your activities honestly, you can see whether you're truly doing the work that leads to deals, or whether you're just filling the day.

And once you see the truth, you can fix it.

Going back to Chapter 7, when you chose your marketing methods, you made decisions about how you were going to generate business. Whatever those methods are, you should be tracking them.

For example, let's say you decide you're going to work the phones.

It's easy for an agent to say, "I tried calling people and it didn't work." But what does that actually mean? Did you make five phone calls? Or did you make fifty?

Those are two very different efforts with two very different outcomes.

If you only made five calls, chances are you won't get any prospects. But if you consistently make fifty calls a day, the odds are very good that eventually someone will turn into a lead.

So start by tracking the activity itself.

How many calls did you make?

How many days in a row did you make those calls?

From there, track the next step in the pipeline.

How many prospects did those calls create? Which ones are short-term prospects who may buy or sell soon? Which ones are long-term prospects who may take action later?

And of course, are they buyers or sellers?

From there, you should also track your appointments.

How many listing appointments did you go on this month? What percentage of those appointments turned into actual listings?

The same applies to buyers.

How many buyers are you working with? How many homes are you showing them?

I knew one agent who tracked this down to a science. He had noticed a pattern in his business. If a buyer saw more than a certain number of homes without making an offer, the odds of them buying soon dropped dramatically.

So he made a strategic decision.

Once a buyer crossed that threshold, he would bring in a junior agent. The junior agent would continue showing homes, and when the buyer finally decided to write an offer, the senior agent would step back in to help close the deal.

His reasoning was simple. If a buyer hadn't made an offer after a certain number of showings, they were either very picky or not truly ready to buy. Rather than spending dozens more hours showing homes himself, he would split the commission with a junior agent and free up his own time to focus on new prospects.

That strategy only worked because he tracked his numbers closely enough to recognize the pattern.

Eventually, all of this activity leads to escrows.

So you should also track how many homes you put into escrow each month, and what percentage of those escrows actually close.

This is an area where many agents make an emotional mistake. They want every escrow to close. And when a deal starts to fall apart, they panic.

After all, that commission check might be the difference between paying the bills or not.

But most experienced agents understand that not every deal will close. There are always surprises in real estate. Inspections uncover problems. Financing falls through. Buyers change their minds.

Most successful agents I know assume that a small percentage of escrows simply won't make it to the finish line. Usually the closing rate is still very high, somewhere around 80 to 90 percent, but they understand that a few deals will fall apart along the way.

And as I've mentioned in other chapters, sometimes walking away from a deal that shouldn't close is far better than forcing it through and dealing with a lawsuit later.

Finally, at the end of the year, you do want to look at the big numbers.

How many homes did you sell?

What was the total value of those homes?

How much money did you actually make?

And, as we discussed in Chapter 10, how much did you spend?

I've met plenty of agents who look very successful on paper. They sold a lot of houses. Their gross commissions look impressive.

But when you dig deeper, you discover they spent so much money on marketing, advertising, and lead generation that the profit wasn't nearly as impressive as it appeared.

That's why tracking matters.

When you consistently track your activities, your conversions, and your expenses, you begin to see patterns. You start to understand what's working, what isn't, and where you should focus your time and money.

And that's when your business stops feeling random.

It starts becoming predictable.

Once you accept that you are your own boss, the next challenge becomes obvious very quickly: staying organized.

There are no shortages of books, systems, and philosophies around organization and productivity. One of the most well-known is *The One Thing* by Gary Keller. It's a solid book. I've read it. I'm a fan. He talks extensively about time blocking, structuring your day so every block of time has a specific purpose.

And for a lot of people, time blocking works incredibly well. I know agents who operate at a very high level because their day is mapped out down to the minute. They know exactly what they're doing at 9:30, 11:00, and 2:15. It's efficient. It's disciplined. It's impressive.

It just doesn't work for me.

I've tried. Multiple times. And for whatever reason, my brain and time blocking simply don't get along. That doesn't mean it's a bad system, it just means it's not *my* system. That's an important distinction, because not everyone's brain is wired the same way. What works brilliantly for one person can be frustrating or ineffective for another.

That's why the real goal isn't to adopt the "right" system. It's to find the system that actually works for you.

I do use an online calendar. I think something like Google Calendar is essential, especially for reminders, appointments, and anything that involves other people. But here's my problem with digital tools: they're easy to ignore. I can close my phone. I can shut my laptop. I can silence notifications. And if I do that, whatever is in my calendar might as well not exist.

What *does* work for me is embarrassingly low-tech.

After years of experimenting, I finally accepted that I need a giant whiteboard next to my desk. Everything goes on it. Yes, most of it is also in my digital calendar, but the whiteboard is always there. I don't have to open anything. I don't have to log in. I can't swipe it away. If I sit at my desk, I see exactly what's coming up.

When I tell people this, some of them think it's ridiculous. Others immediately say, "Why wouldn't you just use an app?" And that's fine. Their system works for them. Mine works for me.

Another tool I resisted for years, but now swear by, is a full one-year wall calendar.

I'd heard about these forever and honestly thought they were unnecessary. I already had a monthly calendar. How different could it really be?

Completely different.

The first year I used a one-year calendar, it was a game changer. Suddenly, nothing was "off the page." Events that were two or three months away weren't hidden in some future month I hadn't flipped to yet. They were always visible. I stopped being surprised by things I had technically scheduled but mentally forgotten.

It also works in reverse. If I'm trying to remember when something happened, I don't have to dig through emails or scroll endlessly. I can glance at the calendar and immediately see whether it was three weeks ago or three months ago.

Will this work for everyone? Absolutely not.

But that's the point.

There are endless books, tools, and systems promising to organize your life and maximize your productivity. I'm not here to tell you which one to use. I'm here to tell you to find one that actually works for *you*, and then stick with it.

Don't worry if someone else thinks your system is strange. Don't worry if it's not trendy. Don't worry if someone makes fun of it. If it keeps you organized, keeps you moving forward, and keeps you accountable in a business where no one else is doing that for you, then it's the right system.

In real estate, effectiveness beats elegance every time.

Another thing I love about the whiteboard is that it gives me a place to capture ideas as they come to me.

Some of those ideas are urgent, things I need to do today or this week. Others are medium-term, like things I want to get to later this month. And some are long-term ideas that aren't important right now but would be easy to forget if I didn't write them down somewhere. Having a place where all of that can live, visibly and without judgment, keeps my brain from constantly trying to remember everything at once.

I usually keep a running list off to the side. It's not fancy. Just a simple collection of things that need attention at some point. Alongside that, I'll have a shorter list for the day, what actually needs to get done *today*.

And I'll admit it: I love crossing things off the list.

There's something deeply satisfying about it. It's tangible proof that you moved something forward, even if the win was small. In a business where results can take weeks or months to show up, those small visible wins matter more than people realize.

That said, there's an important trap here.

Being organized can feel like productivity without actually being productive.

It's very easy to sit down and convince yourself you're "working" by rewriting lists, color-coding calendars, reorganizing notes, or endlessly tweaking your system. Before you know it, an hour, or a whole morning, has gone by, and you haven't called a single prospect. You haven't followed up with anyone. You haven't done anything that actually moves the business forward.

The goal of a list isn't to make you feel organized.

The goal is to make you *do the work.*

Your to-do list should be filled with actions that create momentum: calls made, conversations started, relationships nurtured, problems solved. If you catch yourself spending more time organizing your work than doing your work, it's a sign you've drifted into avoidance, whether you mean to or not.

So use lists. Use calendars. Use whiteboards. Use whatever tools help you stay focused.

Just don't confuse preparation with progress.

At the end of the day, real estate doesn't reward the most organized agent. It rewards the agent who consistently takes action.

CHAPTER 16

The Myths of Work Life Balance

Work-life balance is a term that gets thrown around a lot. It somehow implies that there is a perfect balance, a perfect 50/50 split that can be obtained between your professional life and your home life. The truth? It will never be in perfect balance like a scale. It's more like a seesaw, tilting back and forth, and not always when you're ready.

Work-life balance was best summed up by the business philosopher Jim Rohn, who said:

"When you're at the beach, be at the beach, and don't think about the office. When you're at the office, think about the office, and don't think about the beach."

That is, be intentional about both.

As a real estate agent, or really any real estate professional, the temptation is to work seven days a week. It makes sense. Prospect in the office Monday through Friday. Show houses on Saturday. Sit an open house on Sunday. The pressure to just keep working every single day is strong.

When you're brand new, it even seems logical. There's no income coming in yet, so the instinct is to hustle nonstop. Prospect more. Show more homes. Meet more people. Just keep going.

Early in my career, I didn't really have a defined day off. I simply figured my day off would be whatever day nothing happened to get scheduled. If I had showings on Saturday, then maybe Sunday would end up being the day off. If Sunday was booked with open houses, maybe Monday would be quieter.

Sometimes I would intentionally keep a day open if I knew my wife was taking the kids somewhere interesting and I wanted to join them. But most of the time, I was just playing it by ear.

That system worked fine when business was slow.

The problem came when things got busy, really busy. Suddenly the calendar filled up, and before I knew it, I was working ten or eleven days in a row without even realizing it.

That's when the problems started.

Fatigue sets in. Your brain doesn't think as clearly. Driving from appointment to appointment while exhausted becomes more dangerous. Small mistakes start creeping in. And in real estate, small mistakes can become expensive ones.

Eventually, I had to put my foot down and pick a day that was simply non-negotiable. That was my day off. No exceptions unless there was a true emergency.

I run my inspection company the same way today. Every inspector on the team has an assigned day off that is blocked from the calendar. If we don't do that, the schedule will naturally fill up, and people end up working too many days in a row.

When you're first starting your career, yes, you may need to put in a lot of days. There is a lot to do when you're getting established: prospecting, marketing, building relationships, and learning the business.

But remember this: working yourself into the ground isn't a long-term strategy.

I once had a coach to whom I was explaining how I was struggling to get reports done in a timely manner. I had a million silly excuses. The one and only time he ever yelled at me was when he said:

"If you're doing something, do it with intentionality."

I felt like I had shrunk to being only a few inches tall. I was embarrassed. But I fully deserved to be yelled at. I wasn't being intentional or focusing on my report. I was letting excuses and distractions get in the way. And by taking hours to do something that should take 20–30 minutes, I was losing time with my kids as well. Double ouch!

More simply, when working, focus on getting your work done. Don't get distracted by what kind of background music you'd like to listen to, what beverage would be perfect right now, or what fire is waiting in your email inbox. As Nike would say, "Just do it!"

The same goes for the rest of your life.

I recall when my kids were small, taking them to the playground. Other kids would look at me in awe. I remember one kid saying to my child, "Your dad brings you to the playground? My parents never bring me anywhere," as he ran back to his nanny. It was sad to see how many kids were at the playground with a nanny, and not a parent. I get that parents have to work. My mom was a single working parent. But I also remember feeling like my assorted babysitters raised me more than she did.

However, it's not just about time; it's about being intentional. There were plenty of instances where I had to work, but I also scheduled time after work for playtime. I knew I had to work from, say, 8 to 5, but at 5:30–8, I was all dad. No phone, no email, no distractions.

There is a saying that if it's not in your calendar, it doesn't exist. This goes for your family life. And sometimes you risk getting double-booked. There have been multiple occasions where I told my kids I would be home by 6 and we would do a certain activity as soon as I got home. And then during the day, an awesome opportunity would come up that would help my career or business. But I couldn't. I had to leave that money on the table. All the money in the world can't fix a broken promise to the child who looks up to you the most.

This goes for your spouse or significant other as well. The classic trap a working parent, particularly a father, tends to fall into is the feeling of, "Oh, now we have a kid, I need to work every hour I can." "I need every brownie point I get at work." "I need to take on every project," because getting fired or laid off would be devastating to the family. But in the effort to be the perfect breadwinner, they lose the plot. They let work consume them and ignore the family that is driving them to work so hard. One day, they wake up, and the spouse is gone, and the kids are checked out, all of them tired of feeling abandoned, when they were only set aside in order to provide for them.

Now that my kids are older, planning playtime isn't as important. But planning time is. As a business owner, I tend to be a workaholic. The next sale, the next payroll, the next marketing plan is always on my mind. But I have to schedule the vacation. A few days here, a few days there, and at times, a week off here and a week off there. And when I mean off, I mean off, not checking in with work, going places without cell service. Be intentional about being on vacation.

The goal isn't a perfect split; it's to stop living half-aware in both worlds. If you're working, work with purpose. If you're with your family, be all there. You won't always get it right, I don't. But every time you choose to be intentional, you tip the seesaw toward something better. Don't be the mom pushing her kid on the swing while being on her cell phone, explaining to the person on the other end how she is getting in her quality time with her kid. If you're focused on your phone, it's not really quality time. That's how you build a life you don't need to escape from.

Pick a day off.

Then protect it.

Because if you don't protect your time, no one else will.

CHAPTER 17
Building a Team

At some point in your career, you may start thinking about building something bigger than yourself.

Maybe you imagine having several agents working under you. Maybe you picture running a full real estate team with buyer's agents, assistants, and transaction coordinators. Some agents eventually even dream about opening their own brokerage and managing dozens, if not hundreds, of agents.

Not everyone wants that responsibility, and that's perfectly fine. Plenty of agents build fantastic careers as solo operators.

But if you find yourself thinking about scaling your business, creating something that operates beyond just your personal effort, then eventually you will need to learn how to build a team.

And building a team changes everything.

Because the moment you start bringing other people into your business, you stop being just a salesperson. You become a leader.

You're responsible not only for your own success, but for creating an environment where other people can succeed too.

Most people become real estate agents because they want to avoid the trapped feeling of other careers.

You don't want a factory job doing the same repetitive task over and over. You don't want to sit behind a desk all day, feeling chained to a chair, unable to step away because someone might question whether they're being "productive."

Real estate promises something different. The ability to control your own schedule. The ability to build something for yourself. The ability to create a life that isn't defined by punching a clock.

So in the beginning, most agents attack the job with enthusiasm. You're excited to start a new career. You're motivated. You're working hard and building momentum as a single agent.

But over time, something strange happens.

Your career slowly turns into a job.

You realize that if you stop working, the business stops too. If you go on vacation, the income stops. If you take time off, the pipeline dries up. Suddenly, the freedom that attracted you to real estate starts to feel like a trap.

You don't own a business.

You own a job.

The book *The E-Myth* by Michael E. Gerber explains this problem better than almost anything I've ever read. It describes why so many people who believe they own businesses are actually just self-employed.

When I first read that book, I hated it.

I looked for every possible reason why the author must be wrong. I wanted proof that the book was ridiculous and didn't apply to me.

But eventually, I had to face a hard truth.

The problem wasn't the book.

The problem was me.

I thought I had built a successful business, but what I actually had was a successful job. If I stopped working, money stopped coming in. There was no system. No team. No machine running behind the scenes.

Vacations were especially stressful.

Every time I took time off, it felt like I was stepping away from my mortgage payment. Every day away from work meant money not coming in and opportunities being missed.

Eventually, that started to bother me for another reason.

It wasn't just affecting me. It was affecting my kids.

We rarely went anywhere because I always felt like I had to be working. And that wasn't the life I wanted for them. When I was growing up, my family went to the same place every vacation. It was nice, but after a while, it lost its magic.

Now I was repeating the same pattern in a different way.

Except worse.

We weren't even going anywhere.

That realization forced me to start thinking differently about my business.

If I wanted real freedom, I needed something more than a job.

I needed a team.

And that's where fear starts creeping in.

Almost every agent who considers building a team has the same set of fears.

What if I can't afford an employee?

What if I end up paying them instead of paying myself?

What if they don't do the job as well as I do?

What if I lose control of my business?

These thoughts feel very real when they're bouncing around in your head. But in most cases, they're just stories we tell ourselves to justify staying exactly where we are.

A helpful way to think about fear is this old acronym:

F.E.A.R., False Evidence Appearing Real.

Many of the things we worry about are not actual facts. They're just imagined outcomes that stop us from taking the next step.

Another book that helped me think about this differently is *Procrastinate on Purpose* by Rory Vaden. He suggests that every task you do should fall into one of five categories.

You either eliminate it, automate it, delegate it, concentrate on it, or procrastinate on it until later.

When you look at your work through that lens, something interesting happens. You start realizing how many things you do every day that you probably shouldn't be doing at all.

Some tasks can be eliminated completely. Others can be automated with systems or software. And many tasks can be delegated to someone else.

What remains are the things that truly require your attention, the work that only you can do.

This is where a simple but powerful concept comes into play.

You can always make more money.

But you cannot make more time.

Your time has value. And if you're doing work that could be done for less than your time is worth, then you're actually losing money by doing it yourself.

The math here is surprisingly straightforward.

Start by asking a few basic questions. How many homes do you sell in a year? What is the average commission on those homes? After your broker's split, fees, and expenses, how much are you actually taking home?

Now divide that number by the number of hours you work.

That gives you an approximate hourly value of your time.

Let's say you run the numbers and it comes out to about $60 an hour.

Now think about all the tasks you do in your business that could be handled by someone making $20 an hour.

Every hour you spend doing those tasks is effectively costing you $40 in lost opportunity.

Those are the first things you should consider delegating.

Because the moment someone else takes those tasks off your plate, your time becomes available for the work that actually generates income.

And that's where building a team begins to transform your business.

Another book that shaped my thinking about building a business is *The Entrepreneurial Roller Coaster* by Darren Hardy. It's probably the business book I've read more times than any other. I highly recommend it.

In the book, Darren talks about his time working as a real estate agent. He points out that there are hundreds, maybe thousands, of things an agent can do during the day that feel productive.

Setting up escrow files.
Taking photos of a property.
Ordering property reports.
Scheduling termite inspections.
Meeting with the appraiser.
Attending the home inspection.
Installing the lockbox.
Showing up at closing.

All of these are legitimate tasks. They all feel like real work. And in many ways, they are.

But Darren argues that there are really only three vital functions of a real estate agent:

1. Pitching listings
2. Negotiating contracts
3. Prospecting for new business

In his words, everything else can be delegated.

I've found this to be largely true in my own business.

I started as a one-person operation. Over time, that grew to two people, then three, then four. Today, I have fifteen people on my team, and we're still growing.

The interesting thing is that the more people I hire, the more responsibilities I delegate. And the more I delegate, the more time I have to focus on the things that actually move the business forward: long-term strategy, high-level thinking, and growth.

That shift only happens when you stop trying to do everything yourself.

Earlier in the book, I mentioned another influential idea from *Start With Why* by Simon Sinek. Before you start building a team, you need to understand why you want one.

Do you want to build a large organization?

Do you want the freedom to make money even when you're not personally working every transaction?

Do you want the responsibility, and the challenge, of leading a larger team?

There isn't a single correct answer. But you do need clarity. Because once you understand your "why," you can begin building the structure that supports it.

One area where people often get stuck is the hiring process itself.

Most people think hiring starts with writing a job ad and collecting résumés. Résumés certainly have their place, but I've learned they're often the least interesting part of the hiring process.

A resume tells me where someone has been.

I'm much more interested in where someone is going.

If you looked at my own resume, it would probably look like a mess. There are twists, turns, and detours that don't make much sense on paper. In many ways, the fact that my resume is messy is exactly what pushed me to build something of my own.

That's what I want to understand when I'm hiring someone.

What are they trying to accomplish?

Where do they want to go in life?

Are they ambitious? Are they trying to improve their situation? Are they trying to build a career, support a family, or create opportunities for themselves?

In hiring language, this is often described as identifying someone's pain point.

What problem is this person trying to solve by taking this job?

Do they need stable income to pay rent?

Are they trying to build experience?

Are they working toward college or a long-term career?

If your company can help solve that problem for them, you're much more likely to have a committed and motivated employee.

But if the situation is simply:

"I need someone to work for me."

"I need a job."

That relationship rarely lasts long.

Another mistake I see real estate agents make when building teams is failing to truly invest in their people.

Sometimes an agent gets busy and thinks, "I have more clients than I can handle. I'll just bring on another agent to help show houses or open the door for inspections."

That can work in the short term. But if the new agent isn't learning, growing, and building their own future, they won't stay very long.

No ambitious agent wants to spend their career simply opening doors and running errands for someone else.

When you build a team, you have to give people a reason to stay. That means mentoring them, teaching them, and helping them move forward in their careers.

The real purpose of a team is that you have more business than you can personally handle, and you are capable of generating even more.

That means eventually you will need to hand some of that business to other people.

For many agents, that idea feels uncomfortable.

"I worked really hard to generate these leads. Why would I give them to someone else?"

But that's exactly the point of having a team.

Some people are excellent at generating business. Others are excellent at servicing that business.

In my own company, marketing and servicing are two completely different departments, handled by different people. The inspectors on my team don't want to go out and market the company. They don't want to spend their days networking, shaking hands, and handing out cards.

They want to do inspections.

They look to me to bring in the work.

Which means I have to be willing to hand that work off.

If you don't have enough business, or if you're not willing to share that business, you're probably not ready to build a team yet.

The question is, where to start? For most real estate agents, the first hire usually isn't another agent.

I say start small. Even a part-time person can be golden. My first hire was part-time, 9 a.m. to 2 p.m., just to answer my phone. Over six years later, she's still with me. You don't even have to start that big. Maybe a college student two afternoons a week to help you design flyers and schedule social media posts. I have generally had great luck with stay-at-home moms. They are often highly trained and experienced, but have decided to take themselves out of the full-time workforce. But many want a small job for a few hours a week just to have something to do and earn some spending money in between diaper changes, PTA meetings, and school drop-off and pickup.

Junior agents can sometimes seem attractive because they often work on commission rather than hourly pay. But unless you already have a large pipeline of deals to hand them, that structure can become frustrating for everyone involved.

An hourly team member who handles the administrative work is often far more valuable early on. Yes, you have to pay them regardless of whether the deal closes or not, but they also won't quit because they thought they were getting 1 percent of the deal and now they're not.

Transaction coordinators manage paperwork, contracts, and compliance. Executive assistants can manage your calendar, schedule appointments, answer calls, and keep your business organized.

In many cases, one person can handle several of these responsibilities.

Over time, something interesting begins to happen.

There's an agent I've known for many years, Cindy. When we first met, Cindy was a one-person real estate agent, and I was a one-person inspection company.

As time went on, Cindy built a team. First, an assistant. Then a junior agent. Then I built a team. First, someone to answer phones, then a junior inspector. We both kept adding.

Eventually, we reached the point where it became a funny cliché that actually came true:

"Your people will call my people."

Instead of Cindy calling me directly to schedule an inspection, someone on her team would call someone on my team. One of my inspectors would go out and perform the inspection.

Building a team takes work.

Too many people fall into the trap of believing the old saying, "If you build it, they will come." The idea is that if you just add more people to your organization, the business will somehow appear automatically.

That's not how it works.

Having a larger team does not guarantee more business. What it does is give you the capacity to handle more business.

But the responsibility for generating that business still falls on you as the leader.

You have to keep the pipeline full. You have to keep opportunities coming in, because if there isn't enough work to go around, people will eventually leave, and all the effort you put into building the team will disappear with them.

At the same time, you can't let fear stop you from growing.

One of the most common fears agents have is, "What if I hire someone and I don't have enough business for them?"

Ironically, I've found the opposite tends to happen.

Every time I add someone to my team, it motivates me to work harder, not because I suddenly have more tasks to do, but because I feel responsible for making sure there is enough opportunity for everyone.

That responsibility sharpens your focus.

You stop worrying about minor tasks and start concentrating on the bigger picture. You think more about strategy, growth, and where the next opportunities will come from.

Interestingly, this doesn't necessarily mean you work longer hours.

In many ways, you may actually work less on the day-to-day operations. Instead, your work shifts toward higher-level thinking, long-term planning, and leadership.

You stop being the person doing everything.

You become the person guiding the direction.

And that's the real difference between having a job and building a business.

Final Thoughts

If there's one thing I want you to take away from this book, it's this: never stop learning.

Real estate is one of those professions where the moment you think you've figured it all out is the moment you start falling behind. Markets change. Technology changes. Marketing changes. Consumer expectations change. What worked five years ago might not work today, and what works today may not work five years from now.

I often tell people that if I ever say "because that's the way we've always done it" as a reason not to change, or at least look at something new, then kick me.

Agents that stay successful year after year, decade after decade, don't just go all in. They change and adapt as the world changes. They adopt new technology, new ideas, and stay curious.

And find a mentor, or several. A fatal flaw in thinking is that a mentor has to be one all-inclusive person. It can be several people. Maybe one mentor is good at marketing, while another is good at staying organized. And don't be afraid to change mentors now and then. Some mentors are great at helping you get going, while others may be better at taking someone who's going to new heights.

Ultimately, you have to work on yourself. Business philosopher Jim Rohn had a saying, "If you want to get more, you have to become more." Meaning, you can't just rely on luck, circumstances, or time to get what you want, but you need to change the way your mind works around what you want.

I am always feeding my mind: new books, podcasts, and more from business and thought leaders.

None of us will ever know everything. So don't think of this as the end of the book, but rather the beginning of the next phase of your real estate career.

www.ingramcontent.com/pod-product-compliance
Lightning Source LLC
LaVergne TN
LVHW050915210926
848482LV00012B/448
* 9 7 9 8 9 0 2 5 2 2 0 5 8 *